GUILLAUME DE MACHAUT

Da Capo Press Music Reprint Series

GENERAL EDITOR
FREDERICK FREEDMAN
VASSAR COLLEGE

Guillaume de Machaut

BY SIEGMUND LEVARIE

Edited by John J. Becker

DA CAPO PRESS · NEW YORK · 1969

GUILLAUME DE MACHAUT

NATURE PRESENTS TO MACHAUT HER THREE CHILDREN: REASON, RHETORIC, AND MUSIC (see p. 20).

Guillaume de Machaut

BY SIEGMUND LEVARIE

Great Religious Composers

Edited by John J. Becker

NEW YORK · SHEED AND WARD · 1954

To Paul and Erika Fromm
in whose hospitable country home
this book was begun and finished

Foreword

Guillaume de Machaut lived in the fourteenth century, which produced such men as Dante, Giotto, and Petrarch. Although even the name of Machaut is comparatively little known today, in his own time his renown was equal to theirs.

With one great exception, Machaut's musical compositions were in a secular vein. That one exception—the great Mass with which this book is concerned—is of such magnitude that it alone gives him his position of importance as a church composer. For Machaut's Mass was the first ever to be composed as a polyphonic cycle, in short, the first musical structure of its kind.

This book might have been entitled *Machaut and his Mass*; for it deals with the man in his historical setting and with his one great religious composition, the aesthetic problems it solved, and the structure and symbolism of the music itself.

JOHN J. BECKER, B.M. Mus. D.
Editor
Composer in Residence and
Professor of Music
Barat College of the Sacred Heart
Lake Forest, Illinois

Siegmund Levarie

Siegmund Levarie is both a practicing musician and a musicologist, a dual role which accounts for his performing Machaut's Mass at the University of Chicago in 1951 and his writing about the work and the composer two years later. Levarie's performances of Machaut's works (including many secular songs) with his Collegium Musicum at the University were probably the first in Chicago.

Educated at the University of Vienna and the Vienna Conservatory, Levarie began his career as teacher of music theory and history in the Department of Music and as orchestra conductor at the University of Chicago in 1938. Except for four years service in the United States Army, he was active at the University until 1952 at which time he became Dean of the Chicago Musical College. In the same year he also was appointed director of the Fromm Music Foundation, a newly established organization for the furtherance of contemporary music. Mr. Levarie's immediate future involves taking over the chairmanship of the Department of Music at Brooklyn College and the conductorship of the Brooklyn Community Symphony Orchestra.

Two other books by Mr. Levarie have recently been published: *Mozart's Le Nozze di Figaro. A Critical Analysis* (1952) and *Fundamentals of Harmony* (1954).

J. J. B.

CONTENTS

I. Guillaume de Machaut and His Time   3

II. Problems of a Religious Composer   37

III. Machaut's Mass   73

    Bibliography   111

    Records   114

GUILLAUME DE MACHAUT

I. Guillaume de Machaut and His Time

GUILLAUME DE MACHAUT, composer and poet, was born around 1300 in the village of Machault near Réthel in the Champagne in France and died in 1377 as a canon of Rheims. Chronologically and artistically he represents his century, with which his life almost coincided and from which he emerges as the outstanding creative musician.

The dry facts, "He was born, lived, and died," are of no distinction unless related to the specific forces around them. The particulars of Machaut's life, as we know them from his own writings as well as from other witnesses, will shine more clearly after we have quickly thrown a light on the political, religious, and artistic situation of his generation.

A mere enumeration of contemporaneous events leaves little doubt about the physical and spiritual tension of his day. France was involved in a miserable war with England, which, fought entirely on French soil, lasted a "Hundred Years." As if the violence of the war were not killing enough

people, the Black Plague struck France in the middle of the
fighting and of the century. The Popes, losing their struggle
for secular as well as religious sovereignty, had to abandon
Rome and live in "Babylonian captivity" in the south of
France. Religious thought permeated almost all phases of
daily life. The big Gothic cathedrals of France had just
been built. Parisians, then as now, worshipped underneath
the vast vault of Notre Dame and, on special occasions
reserved for privileged people, amidst the intimate colored
windows of Sainte-Chapelle. They could also study at the
Sorbonne, which had received its name from Robert de
Sorbon, the confessor of the sainted king Louis IX. Amidst
the external and impersonal violence, humanistic art sud-
denly blossomed. Dante's vision initiated the century.
Petrarch, Boccaccio, Chaucer, and Giotto achieved individualized expression of a spiritual power that, unlike the
political upheavals, has never lost its direct impact on our
civilization. To their ranks belonged the poet and musician
Machaut, who, among composers known by name, was without peer in any country.

This enumeration of events deserves a fuller description.
In terms of their influence on Machaut's life, we need not
investigate the many causes of the Hundred Years' War
between England and France—the vanity of ruling families,
the disintegration of feudalism (in favor of a constitutional
sovereign in England, of an autocrat in France), the rivalry
for commercial gains in the trade with the Low Countries,
and a chain of personal irritants. What interests us here is
the possible effect of the political turmoil on a composer

exposed to it. The conflict, which had been simmering throughout Machaut's youth, broke out into the open when he was in his thirties. In 1337, King Edward III of England invaded Flanders; and for the remainder of Machaut's life, the French people, of whom he was one, were losing ground, life, and honor. Although the actual fighting was intermittent and hostilities were interrupted by frequent truces, misery and danger were the daily companions of the French. The one major respite of the war occurred in the decades following Machaut's death.

How the war appeared to Machaut may be elucidated by some authentic reports. Jean de Bueil, famous as a soldier and as the author of a kind of military textbook, *Le Jouvencel*, writes: "In going my way, I found myself in a very desolate and deserted country, because there had been war between the inhabitants of the country for a long time, and they were very poor and few in number; for, I may tell you, it seemed rather a place for wild beasts than a habitation for people."[4] The conflict of interests was not restricted to that of the two kings. "The storm of civil war," writes the chronicler Jean Chartier, "rose everywhere; between the children of the same house, between men of the same rank were committed the outrages of cruel wars; the multiplied wars of the lords became mixed up in these conflicts."[17]

Two big battles between the English and the French, fought around the middle of the century when Machaut was writing his Mass, ended in disaster for his side. At Crécy in 1346, "there was a very hard struggle and wonderful fight. The English archers were in ambush behind the hedges and, with their volley, killed many horses and men. And on this day men were killed by horses; for as the French were thinking to range themselves, their horses were falling dead. What need to prolong the story? By hastiness and disarray were the French discomfited."[8] Among the thirty thousand reportedly slain was the old Count of Luxemburg, the King of Bohemia, John the Blind. He had been Machaut's benevolent employer for over two decades. The composer doubtless suffered from this blow.

At Poitiers, ten years later, "the clamour and uproar were heard more than three leagues away. And there was great sorrow to see the flower of all nobility and knighthood thus given over to destruction . . . By force was taken King John of France."[8] When he bought his liberty after four years of imprisonment at the price of half his kingdom, the road from Calais to Paris was so infested with bandits that the King had to negotiate a safe conduct from them. "A lamentable thing," Petrarch writes about this incident, "and truly shameful! The King himself, on his return from captivity, found obstacles to his re-entry into the capital. He was forced to treat with the brigands. Posterity will refuse to believe it."[17] These events must have been felt by Machaut, who lived amidst them. To help defray the expenses of the war, the clergy of France were frequently taxed by agreement of the French Popes and the French kings. Machaut must have been liable to a form of income tax. The law passed shortly after the defeat at Poitiers established a progressive tax but with a backward progression. An income of a thousand pounds was liable to a tax of two percent; an income of ten pounds, to one of ten percent.[17] We need only imagine ourselves in the role of a contemporary observer to experience some emotional pangs that may not have been foreign to Machaut: "In 1363 were seen only the crushing and oppression of the people . . . not only by the brigands but by the heavy impositions and taxes. What murders in the villages and woods! The people found no defenders. Quite the opposite, the aristocracy seemed pleased at the prevalence of these evils, to which they should have applied a remedy with diligent hands."[17]

One year after Machaut had lost his benefactor, the King of Bohemia, in the battle of Crécy, a terrible onset of the bubonic plague began to ravage France. The "Black Death" had been imported from Asia to the port of Genoa. The opening pages of Boccaccio's *Decamerone* describe the devastation, be it Florence or Paris: "There was not a day that thousands of them did not fall sick, who, through not being helped or succoured in any way, nearly all died. And there were quite a number who died in the streets, day and night; and others who died in their houses first made their neighbors aware that they were dead by the stench of their decaying corpses." In towns like Avignon, the residence of the Popes, "there died in one day one thousand three hundred and twelve persons, according to a count made for the Pope."[25] In Paris, eight hundred people died daily. When famine hit Europe in 1348, the *Chronicle* of Froissart computes that "the third part of the world" perished by the double scourge.[16]

Machaut was deeply touched by the calamities around him. In the opening pages of *Le Jugement dou Roy de Navarre*, a long allegoric poem written in 1349, he gives vent to his feelings in words of sincere melancholy.[32] He is alone in his chamber and grieves that justice and truth have died. Avarice rules supreme. Everybody tries to cheat and deceive: father, son, daughter, sister, brother, mother, godmother, cousin, aunt, uncle, neighbor, neighboress, husband, wife, friend, sweetheart bring destruction on one another without pity and compassion. Never in history has he read of such hard and horrible perils as those of his own time. Five hundred thousand men and women lose body and soul because of the war, and nobody cares. The Jews are being cruelly persecuted—hanged, broiled, drowned, and beheaded. Many Christians lose their minds and madly flagellate themselves as if they could thereby reach paradise. When Nature sees that man is so destroying her work, she summons the four winds to spread horror and disease over the earth. The plague kills so many people that nobody can count their number, nor imagine, think, name, compute, deduce, or describe it. Machaut expresses his thoughts, but who is there to know them, "comment qu'assez de mes amis Fussent mors et en terre mis." Most of his friends are dead and buried.

The plague had subsided, but the general situation was much the same when Charles V, the son of John who had been captured at Poitiers, was crowned king of France in

1364. Machaut's Mass, allegedly written for the occasion, remains associated with the event. The most splendid Mass of the age, it might well have been performed at the coronation, although not for the first time. The King "understood so well every aspect of music, which is the science of harmonizing sounds by slow and fast notes, . . . that no discord could pass unperceived by him."[38] He was on intimate terms with the composer. When Charles journeyed to Rheims a few years before the coronation, he advised the aldermen of the town to meet him at his lodgings "chez maistre Guillyaume de Machault."[32] A subtle interpretation of certain passages in Machaut's works persuades us that he was employed by the gentle King in some capacity, probably as a secretary.[32] Once he calls the King his rightful Lord by whom he has been nourished, his "droit Signeur . . . Car fais suis de sa nourriture, Et suis sa droite créature."[38] The King, a generation younger than Machaut, deserved his surname, "The Wise," if we judge him by his interest in arts and letters. It was he who rebuilt the old fortress of the Louvre to give it the storybook aspect, full of terraces and turrets, well known from an illustration in the *Book of Hours* of his brother, the Duke John of Berry. It was he who ordered Aristotle's *Ethics* and *Politics* to be translated from Latin into French. These accomplishments, so encouraging to a spirit like Machaut's, were matched by his support of the new art of artillery. In his reign, French cannon were made which were capable of throwing stone bullets weighing a hundred pounds.[17]

Charles V was still alive when Machaut died in 1377. The

impact of the composer's death was felt less than the simultaneous deaths of two ruling political figures. Edward III
of England, who had willfully pursued the war from its
beginnings, was succeeded by a ten-year-old child, Richard
II, whose downfall at the end of the century is well known
to us through Shakspere's tragedy. In Avignon, the French
Pope Gregory XI died. A conclave in Rome elected an
Italian, Urban VI, as his successor; but a new conclave
in the Kingdom of Naples gave Robert of Geneva the tiara,
which he assumed under the name of Clement VII. Charles V
supported the latter, the University of Paris the former;
and the Great Schism, which split Europe in half, lasted
until 1415.

The religious sphere around Machaut must have influenced his life and thought as much as the political. The big
external event is the physical presence of the Popes in
France. Their exile from Rome in Avignon, on the banks
of the Rhone, a safe distance inland from the mouth of
the river, coincides with Machaut's century. At the time of
the composer's birth, Philip IV, the Fair, was king. A contemporary, the lawyer and politician Guillaume de Nogaret,
praises the King's humility and modesty. "He is never angry.
He hates no one; he is jealous of none; full of grace and
charity; pious, merciful; pursuing at all times truth and
justice."[17] This is the same King who, letting his need of
money dictate his policy, raided the hoards of the Jews and
the Lombard bankers; debased the coinage; allowed the
serfs of the royal domain to commute their services for
money payments; confiscated the vast treasures of the Mili-

tary Order of Knights Templars before dissolving the Order and burning alive the Grand Master Jacques de Molay; and extorted money from every institution and class in his dominions.[35] He did not spare the clergy. When Pope Boniface VIII issued a bull *Clericis Laicos* forbidding secular princes to tax the clergy, Philip the Fair struck back by closing the export of gold and silver from France, thus drying up a main source of the Papal revenues. Boniface VIII's thirst for gold assigns to him, even before his actual death, a place in the Inferno of his Florentine contemporary, Dante, at the bottom of the third chasm (Canto XIX): "Are you already there, Boniface, are you already there? Are you yet satisfied with those riches for which you prostituted the Church?"

The details of the struggle are less relevant to our interest in Machaut than the outcome. Philip won every round. When the Papal chair was left vacant in 1305, the Archbishop of Bordeaux, elected to occupy it as Clement V, abandoned Rome for Avignon. Throughout Machaut's life, the Popes lived in French Provence, virtual prisoners of a secular power.

Their physical presence may be taken as a symbol of the permeation by religion of almost all activities of the daily life in France. "There is not an object nor an action, however trivial, that is not constantly correlated with Christ or salvation. All thinking tends to religious interpretation of individual things; there is an enormous unfolding of religion in daily life."[24] One startling illustration may here take the place of a detailed list. The cloister of the churchyard of

the Innocents at Paris, which was torn down in the seventeenth century, was frequented by Machaut's contemporaries
as a sort of counterpart of the Palais Royal of 1789 or of a
public park or market of today. Preferred by rich and poor
to every other place of burial, the churchyard was hand-
somely adorned by sculptures and paintings. Machaut's benefactor, the Duke of Berry, commissioned statues to be
carved for the portal. In order to clear space, skulls and
bones were frequently dug up and, in heaps along the
cloisters enclosing the ground on three sides, lay open to the
eye by thousands. Day after day, crowds of people prome-
naded under the cloisters. "In spite of the incessant burials
and exhumations going on, it was a public lounge and a
rendezvous. Shops were established before the charnel-
houses and prostitutes strolled under the cloisters. A female
recluse was immured on one of the sides of the church,
Friars came to preach and processions were drawn up there
. . . Even feasts were given there."[24]

The political misery and religious tension of Machaut's
century proved not averse to creative sensitivity. Are we sur-
prised to find art blossoming under the heels of war, famine,
and pestilence? It has always been so, and our own century
makes no exception. Composers and poets rather than gen-
erals and kings are responsible for the continuity of our
civilization. The religious tension, in particular, could easily
find an outlet in sensual activities. "Amor spiritualis facile
labitur in nudum carnalem amorem," goes the diagnosis of
Jean Gerson, the religious chancellor of the Paris university,
about the turn of the new century. Spiritual love easily be-

comes worldly love. The wonderful *dulcedo Dei*, the sweetness experienced through God, might be a temptation of the devil.[24] To the historian of the late Middle Ages, the inseparability of the religious and secular spheres is expressed in the liveliest manner by the fact that profane melodies might be used indiscriminately for sacred purposes, and sacred for profane.[24] Machaut did not hesitate to build a passionate motet (Nr. 10), "Hareu! le feu d'ardant desir," on a Gregorian tenor, "Christus factus est pro nobis obediens usque mortem," of which the phrase "obedient unto death" is used to interpret the lover's declaration; or to combine in another motet (Nr. 17) an ardent love poem addressed to his "pucellette maistrie" with a tenor on the Gregorian melody of "Ave regina."[28] One century after him and heir to his culture, Guillaume Dufay composed Masses to the themes of love songs, such as "Tant je me déduis" ("So much I enjoy myself"), "Se la face ay pale" ("If my face is pale"), and "L'homme armé" ("The armed man"). This blurred distinction between spiritual and temporal matters could become responsible for the unleashing of new humanistic forces. It could, of course, easily turn to irreverence. Choristers did not scruple to sing the profane words of the songs into the Mass which was built on their themes: "Baisez-moi" ("Kiss me"), "Rouges nez" ("Red noses").[24]

Irreverent but popular among Machaut's contemporaries was Boccaccio, whose *Decamerone* describes old topics with a new spirit. His compatriot Petrarch, with whom the French themselves compared Machaut, reveals a great force of mind in his poems and treatises. But he is also known as one of the first modern men to climb a mountain for the earthly pleasure of it. From the top of his favorite Mont Ventoux, he could see down the Rhone valley the steep ramparts of the new Papal palace in Avignon. On a chapel wall in the Palazzo del Bargello in Florence, Giotto, "the master by whom the true art of painting was recovered," painted a likeness of his friend Dante. Machaut was not alone in the artistic realm of his times, nor was he unrecognized. Chaucer's literary debt to Machaut (who, one must not forget, was a poet as well as a composer) is so well acknowledged that he has been referred to as the Frenchman's disciple. His "Legende of Good Women" interweaves phrases and lines derived from the French poet. Whether the two ever met in person is subject to a pleasant speculation. Chaucer fought with the English army in France in 1359-60 and was taken prisoner near Rheims, where Machaut was living as a canon of the cathedral. He may well have paid his respects to the famous and older master.

Against the political, religious, and artistic background of the fourteenth century, Machaut's life may appear in more vivid outline. He was born about 1300. The editor of his works (whose definitive guidance we here follow) believes that Machaut was of humble birth because the documents never mention his origin.[32] Machaut once refers to himself as a "clerc." In other documents he is called "maître," a title suggesting that he had received the degree of *magister* (master of theology, we would say today) at the university. Either because of the ecclesiastical garb or his artistic genius, he soon found himself in the good company of the highest men in the country. His first patron was the colorful John of Luxemburg, King of Bohemia, whom Carlyle described as a "restless, ostentatious, far-grasping, strong-handed man, who kept the world in a stir wherever he went."[7] He went all over Europe—from Lithuania to Italy, and from Poland to France—and took Machaut with him after meeting the young man in Paris in 1323. Certain documents in the Vatican archives tell us of various benefices obtained by the King of Bohemia for Machaut, "pro . . . familiari et domestico, notario, secretario suo."[42] From 1333 to his death in 1377, Machaut held a canonicate at Rheims, where the kings of France were traditionally consecrated. His ecclesiastical position did not interfere with his journeys and other duties toward his worldly patrons. The Papal dispensation was commonly obtained by people less exalted than the King of Bohemia. Details of Machaut's life must be pieced together from trivial as well as historical events. We know that he sold a horse in 1340.[32]

King John of Bohemia, blind, insisted on being led into the battle of Crécy in 1346, "assez avant pour n'en plus revenir."[10] His glorious death in the cause of the French aristocracy forced Machaut to look for another royal patron. Charles II, King of Navarre, proved the most attractive for about a decade. When he earned the surname "the Bad," by allying himself with the English, Machaut left him to cast his lot with the house of France. He probably found various employers; there is a record of a payment of three hundred crowns to Machaut by Amadeus VI, Count of Savoy.[32] But his most important connection was with the highest royal

Lendit, the lovers spend several days together.[38] After making their devotions they find themselves in a little town called La Chapelle. It is June. They are tired from the crowd and the noon heat. A man rents them a room with two beds, "une belle chambrette A .ii. lis, qui est assés nette." The blinds are drawn. Peronnelle's sister-in-law, who has come along, sleeps in one of the beds. "Ma dame en l'autre se coucha, Et .ii. fois ou .iii. me hucha." Machaut is ordered to lie down in the other between Peronnelle and her maid. "On m'efforce!" he cries out. She requests to be kissed, and he tries to reconcile bashfulness with desire, embraces with *honneur*. They continue to live on intimate and gay terms for the remainder of the trip. Later Peronnelle marries another man closer to her age, but the poet resolves to revere her in his art till the end of his days.

He died in April 1377 and was buried in the cathedral of Rheims. His fame remained alive. Eustache Deschamps, a prolific poet in his own right, professed that Machaut had nourished him with much sweetness. He dedicated two ballades to the memory of Machaut, "the flower of flowers of all melody," "the God of harmony on this earth," whose death will be mourned by princes and kings because "his song gave much pleasure to nobles, ladies, and bourgeois."[32] Deschamps' eulogy may be tinged by his personal relation to Machaut, whose disciple and perhaps nephew he was. But he is by no means alone in his exalted praise. For almost a hundred years after Machaut's death—a long survival of literary fame in the Middle Ages—one finds his name listed in one breath with the best authors like Philippe de Vitry,

Alain Chartier, Boccaccio, and Petrarch. He is credited with the invention of new forms as well as the perfection of love songs. Froissart and Christine de Pisan honor Machaut by the most convincing flattery of copying some of his writings without indicating the source of their inspiration.[32]

His fame spread also geographically outside France. Twelve years after his death, Queen Yolande of Catalonia thanks her cousin, the Count de Foix, for sending her a "libre molt bell é bo de Guillem Maixaut." Although no compositions by Machaut have been found in Spain, he must have been well known there; for Spanish nobles were eager to obtain copies of his works from France. The author of a fifteenth-century hunting book in Portugal praised the noise of the hounds by stating that not even Guillaume de Machaut made such a beautiful concordance of melody. "Guilherme de Machado nom fez tam fermosa concordança de melodia, nem que tam bem pareça como a fazem os cañes quando bem correm."[28] The compliment probably worked both ways (as Williams points out).[45] In Italy, around 1400, Ugolino of Orvieto dedicates a whole chapter to Machaut and calls him singular in the discipline of music, one of the best composers, whose songs continue to be used because they are well done and adorned with sweetest sounds.[32] Machaut's influence can be traced by references to his works as well as by the distribution of his scores throughout Europe. Cyprus, at one end, and Poland, at the other, were under his influence. Copies of his works reached cities across the continent, from Strasbourg to Prague and Stockholm.

We perceive various aspects of the role of music in the

lifetime of Guillaume de Machaut. Music represented a philosophic conviction to creative spirits. It brought amusement to society. It became a tool of religion.

The philosophic conviction of a composer must often be deduced from carefully selected clues. Machaut, as skilled with words as with notes, has left us an explicit statement of his artistic aims. Toward the end of his life he wrote a *Prologue*—a preface, we would say today—to the most complete collection of his manuscripts.[32] He personally supervised the arrangement of the collection with a self-consciousness that may well be the cause for the survival of almost all his works. When he promised his lady-friend Peronne a complete edition of his works ("toutes les choses . . . que je fis onques"), he mentioned the existence of more than twenty copies, "car je l'ay fait faire pour aucun de mes seigneurs." They served as presents to important members of the society of his day.[33] His contemporary Petrarch acted with equal concern for his own poetry. Compare this attitude with Bach's lack of apprehension for the fate of his creations and fame.

Machaut's *Prologue* is in the form of an allegory. Nature and Love visit Machaut, present him with certain gifts, and set him various tasks. Nature's gifts are her three children: Reason, Rhetoric, and Music,* Love's three children are Sweet Thinking, Pleasure, and Hope. These personifications are in line with the truly medieval representations of virtues and sins in human shape. Allegory was a favorite poetic medium in Machaut's time; the success of the *Roman de la Rose* with its figures of Dame Leisure, Gaiety, Sweet

* See frontispiece.

Thought, Sweet Speech, and others was universal. One can wonder about the borderline between these images and the freshly revived nymphs, satyrs, and spirits of the Renaissance. The spheres of origin differ, but their fantastic values are the same; and the costumes of the persons around the Rose remind Huizinga of the flowery creations by Botticelli.[24]

Music is a gift of Nature. Machaut proudly suggests an analogy between the creative powers of Nature and those of himself. Nature has formed Guillaume to the end that he, in turn, may form new compositions. Love lends him inspiration. He should be gay, for a sad heart cannot sing well. Music is a science which makes one laugh and sing and dance. "Et Musique est une science Qui vuet qu'on rie et chante et dance." Song is born from gladness, because the essence of joy is musical or harmonious. Nature builds in perfect proportions, and so does music. Hence the universe is fundamentally musical. Music and musical instruments, in turn, follow natural laws and reveal perfect proportion better than anything else on earth. In courtly society, music presides over the dance. In church, men praise God in song. But saints, angels, and archangels also sing praises to God, because He has set them in glory, and they see Him face to face. Hence there is music in paradise. "Donc est Musique en paradis."

Music seems to be the favorite child of Nature; for sixty-two lines are devoted to her praise in the pertinent section of the *Prologue* as compared to a total of twenty-two allotted jointly to Rhetoric, Reason, and the three children of Love. Only Rhetoric receives more than a brief mention.

The idea of perfect proportion lies at the center of all medieval aesthetics. Three things, says St. Thomas Aquinas, are required for beauty: first, integrity or perfection, because what is incomplete is therefore ugly; next, true proportion or consonance; finally, brightness, because whatever has a brilliant color is called beautiful.[2] On such philosophic premises, beauty could be analyzed. But neither Machaut nor any of his contemporaries care to delve below the surface of experience. Denis the Carthusian writes a treatise on beauty. Herbs are beautiful, he says, because they are green; precious stones, because they sparkle; the human body, the dromedary and the camel, because they are functional; the earth, because it is long and wide; the heavenly bodies, because they are round and light.[24]

Anyone first familiarizing himself with medieval aesthetics might feel apprehensive before a system that links music with rhetoric or arithmetic. He will lose his apprehension by studying the long tradition of music as a liberal art. He may be temporarily assuaged by reading in Machaut's letters to Peronnelle that the composer valued the ear as much as the mind, sentiment as much as theory. He writes: "My sweetheart, I have composed the rondel which contains your name and I would have sent it by this messenger; but by my soul, I have never listened to it and I am not accustomed to sending off anything I compose before I have listened to it."[33] In another letter he says: "There is nothing so just and true as experience." He continues by quoting from one of his earlier works: "Qui de sentement ne fait, Son dit et son chant contrefait."[33] He who does not create out of real feeling, counterfeits his words and songs.

Denis the Carthusian himself, whose treatise attempted to intellectualize beauty, is not immune to the sensuous power of music, although he instantly translates the consciousness of beauty into religion. He once entered the church of Saint John in Hertogenbosch while the organ was playing. The sweet melody transported him into a prolonged ecstasy.[24]

The beauty of music, and of art in general, was readily translated into a religious experience. It was also often understood in symbolic terms. In the Middle Ages, a symbolist attitude was prevalent in all thinking and living. The whole world unfolded itself within a vast symbolic context —"a cathedral of ideas," Huizinga calls it, "the richest rhythmic and polyphonic expression of eternal harmony". . . Symbolism is a sort of short-circuit of thought. Instead of looking for the relation between two things by following the hidden detours of their causal connections, thought makes a leap and discovers their relation not in a connection of cause or effects, but in a connection of signification or finality . . . White and red roses are blooming among thorns. The medieval mind at once establishes a symbolic assimilation: virgins and martyrs shine with glory in the midst of their persecutors. How is this assimilation produced? The attributes are the same: the beauty, tenderness, purity, and color of the roses are also those of the virgins and martyrs."

The symbolic force of music pertained, as many a medieval

writer stated, to all things and thoughts. The numerical relations of musical intervals determined the circling of the planets. The harmony of a motet made by men was the image of the harmony of the spheres made by God. The same basic numbers recurred in the crystallization of rocks, in the morphology of plants, and in the structure of man's soul. There are seven tones to a musical scale or mode. They correspond, in a system of symbolic assimilation, to the seven virtues, the seven supplications of the Lord's Prayer, the seven gifts of the Holy Spirit, the seven beatitudes, and the seven penitential psalms. These clusters of seven are again connected with the seven moments of the Passion and the seven sacraments. Each number within each group of seven corresponds as a countermeasure to one of the seven deadly sins, which in turn are represented by seven animals followed by seven diseases.[24]

This symbolic attitude will have to be remembered in the chapter dealing with certain technical niceties of Machaut's Mass. A good example of symbolism is supplied by Williams' discussion of one of Machaut's shorter (and still unprinted) compositions, the Lai XVI.[45] A lai was a definite poetic form. Machaut's disciple Deschamps describes it as long and difficult: "C'est une chose longue et malaisée à faire et à trouver."[12] Machaut's Lai XVI is dedicated to the Virgin. The mystery of the Virgin's relation to the Holy Trinity is artistically expressed by both the text and the music. A metaphor of a fountain assimilates the spout to God the Father, the jet of water to the Son, and the forthcoming stream to the Holy Ghost. The metaphor evokes the traditional ideas of the water of life and the washing away of sins. Musically, the composition is a canon for three voices: the same melody is sung by three voices, entering three long time beats apart. The mysterious oneness of the Trinity finds a perfect symbolic expression in this three-part composition gained from one melody—Three in One.

Not only compositions but also musical instruments lent themselves readily to a symbolic interpretation and enjoyment. The psalter (called in Italy *testa di porco*) symbolized the body of Christ. Because it was straight on all sides, it could also allegorize the even way to God. The tones are produced on the upper part of the psalter, and therefore the spirit is directed upward.[5] On the cithara, the strings cross the sound board. It was because it symbolized the cross that David's cithara drove out Saul's evil spirit. The curves of the sound box of the cithara, moreover, depict the tortuous way to God. The timpani are made of a stretched animal membrane and hence represent the crucifixion of the flesh. St. Augustine compares the trumpet with those who like Job bear suffering patiently, because the metal of the trumpet is subjected to prolonged beating. It was a doctrine of the Neo-Platonists that man himself is an instrument on which God plays.[11]

In Machaut's time, art and music were still wrapped up in life. Their task was to beautify the daily life. Music was not reserved, as it is now, for special moments of elevation. Rather it was used to add intensification and splendor to routine matters, whether religion, chivalry, trade, or love. In a society that considered pomp essential and that identified glamor with beauty, music accompanied many daily activities. For an illustration we can follow Machaut's own words. At the end of his poem *Remede de Fortune*, the lover is reunited with his lady and her friends.[32] They spend a pleasant morning in a manner befitting the polite society of the day. The lady tells Machaut: "Danciez avec nous!" Dance with us! After a while she suggests that he sing a virelay. He obliges with three lilting strophes, introduced and separated from each other by a rhythmically bouncing refrain. Although the song is probably unaccompanied, it inspires a girl of the company to dance to it. There are more songs and amorous pleasantries before the whole group walks to a chapel to attend Mass. At the end of the service, Machaut hears a loud trumpet. Dinner is ready. "But who comes after eating but the musicians, without mishap, all combed and dressed up. They made many different accords. For I saw there in one group viol, rebec, gittern, lute, Moorish guitar, small psalter, citole, and the big psalter, harp, drum, trumpets, kettledrums, organs, horns (more than ten pairs), cornemuses, flageolets, chevrettes, dulzainas, cymbals, bells, timbrel, the Bohemian flute, and the big German cornet, flutes, fistula, pipe, bagpipe, little trumpet, trombones, portatives, monochord where there is only one string, and musette —all together. And certainly, it seems to me that never was such melody seen or heard, for each of them, according to the sound of his instrument, without discord, viol, gittern, citole, harp, trumpet, horn, flute, pipe, souffle, bagpipe, kettledrum, drum, and whatever one can do with finger, quill, and bow, I have seen and heard on this floor.

"After they had danced an estampie, the ladies and their companions went away, in twos and threes, holding fingers, to a very beautiful chamber. And there was no one, man or woman, wanting to be amused, to dance, sing, be entertained at tricktrack, checkers, parsons [part singing?], by games, by notes or by sounds, who did not find there continuously all amusement ready for his wish. And there were musicians, so much better and more learned in the old and new fashion than Music herself who fashions songs, that Orpheus himself, who sang so well that he enchanted all those of the underworld by the sweetness of his singing, would not dare sing before them. When we had been together for a long time, one of the knights merrily called for wine and spices. I think it was his office, for without delay at that moment came the servants.

"After one had eaten the spices and drunk the red wine, noon passed. Three o'clock came. It was now agreed to take leave. Every man and woman left according to common custom. But I lingered behind, as if I were in the clouds, because of my sweet gentle lady whom I saw to be there."

In another poem, *Prise d'Alexandrie*, Machaut describes the festivities accompanying the visit of the King of Cyprus to Prague. The castle was turned into "paradise on earth. There they had all instruments." And to protect himself against the accusation of untruthfulness, the poet recites all instruments by name. The list runs through twenty-one verses and identifies thirty-five different instruments (a modern orchestra seldom contains more than twenty), most of them in the plural. The flute, for instance, is represented in more than ten pairs, that means twenty samples, loud and soft. Even a monochord was there, "which harmonizes with all instruments." The bells begin to ring and make "such noise that it was a marvel. The King marveled very much and said that in his life had he never experienced such great melody."[34]

Music, then as now, could be turned into social entertainment of a rather low order. Festivities occurred in which the musicians had to dress up as animals. Boars blew the trumpets, goats sang a motet, wolves played the flute, and four large donkeys appeared as singers. Some of these reports date from the period after Machaut's death, but we mention them because the social attitude toward music had not changed fundamentally. We read, for instance, of a banquet at which the orchestra of twenty-eight players was placed in a pie.

Once Machaut sent Peronne the music for a song she had ordered. "By God, it is a long time since I have made such a good thing to my taste; and the melodies (*tenures*) are as gentle as fine pap." He added a suggestion: "Whoever performs it on organs, bagpipes, or other instruments, that is its proper nature!"[33] Imagine Ravel sending a song to a friend and suggesting that it be performed by any available combination of instruments! Hindemith, to name another twentieth-century composer, has done so; he has also repeatedly and deliberately paid his respects to Machaut and to performance practices of earlier centuries. The lack of concern for the specific timbre in which a score may be realized is characteristic of old music in general. What mattered were the relationships of pitches and rhythms. These form the essence of a composition. The specific solution in the performance of a composition was incidental. Pieces could be sung, or played, or both sung and played. Organs, bagpipes, stringed instruments, wind instruments— none contradicted the "proper nature" of a composition.

Nor did it matter at what pitch a Machaut ballade might be sung. The manuscripts suggest a tenor range for most of his songs. Yet Peronne, an alto or soprano, sang them; for she writes her lover: "And please send me some of your songs as often as you can; for when I have yours, I have no desire to sing any others."[38]

Recently two ballades by Machaut were identified in a fifteenth-century transcription, or rearrangement, for a keyboard instrument, probably an organ.[39] This fact speaks not only for Machaut's popularity but primarily for the independence of old music from the rigidity of only one specific solution. The underlying philosophic attitude is not indifference to sound but subordination of sound to spirit.

As long as the different parts of a Machaut composition could be clearly differentiated, the listeners were satisfied. The melody lines were not meant to be blended but rather to be sharply profiled. Let no one think that the performances heard by Machaut were therefore of a low standard. His contemporary Jacobus of Liége writes in the book *Speculum Musicae,* a kind of critical encyclopedia of music in the fourteenth century: "I think in all fairness that the modern musical instruments are by far more perfect (*per-*

fecciores) than those that were used in the past when simple
and modest music was the rule. I also think that modern
singers and performers are much better than former ones."[20]

This compliment to the high quality of the performers in
Machaut's time really hides a severe criticism of the complex and immodest style that made them necessary. Jacobus
of Liége was alarmed by the modern manner of composition, by the *ars nova*, with its syncopations, its fast notes,
and its neglect of the sacred triple rhythm. The old style,
the *ars antiqua*, was his ideal. Machaut may have tried to
please both the conservative and the modern elements of
his audience, particularly in the Mass, as we shall find out.
But he must have felt attacked by Jacobus of Liége's widely
read treatise. There were two camps. Philippe de Vitry, a
musician and church dignitary like Machaut, had come out
emphatically for the new style, the *ars nova*. So had
Johannes de Muris, who held a chair of musicology, as we
would say today, at the Sorbonne. But the conservative forces
could apply political pressure on a public figure like
the canon of Rheims. Neither the vast middle classes nor
the Church approved of modern music. Machaut's new
style developed under the protection of the court and the
nobility, as did the individualized music of Dufay and
Ockeghem a century later. But the tranquil circles of the
devout burghers disapproved of polyphony and even of
organs. The rule of Windesheim forbade any embellishment
in vocal music; and even a century after the introduction of
the new style, the *ars nova*, by Machaut and some of his
contemporaries, Thomas à Kempis writes: "If you cannot

sing like the lark and the nightingale, then sing like the
ravens and the frogs in the mire, which sing as God meant
them to."

The strongest opposition to any new expression in the
art of composing came from the Church. St. Thomas
Aquinas had raised the question whether God should be
praised with song at all.[2] Although he reaches the conclusion
that the use of music in the divine praises is a salutary institution, many serious and forceful objections have to be
overcome. Jerome had said that God is to be sung not
with the voice but with the heart. But the praise of the
heart is hindered by singing because the attention of the
singers is distracted from devotion. Easing the throat and
jaws with medicaments makes the church resound with
theatrical measures, and instruments rather move the soul
to pleasure than create a good disposition within it. Denis
the Carthusian, who died in the same year as Thomas
à Kempis, about a century after Machaut had written his
Mass, still had not become accustomed to the introduction
of the modern polyphonic music into the service. Breaking
a melody into small notes (*fractio vocis*) is indicative of a
broken soul. It is comparable to frizzed hair in a man or
pleated dresses in a woman—vanity, nothing else. Certain
people who had participated in polyphonic singing had
confessed to him that they had thereby experienced a certain pride and "lasciviousness of the spirit." Melodies, he
recognizes, may stimulate contemplation and devotion, and
the Church is therefore right in tolerating organs. But when
artful music tickles the ear and begins to amuse the audi-

ence, particularly the women, then it becomes as dangerous
as sin.[24] Ascetic and ecstatic elements, both profoundly religious, were here opposed within the realm of music.

The Church, one must remember, found itself in a peculiar crisis during Machaut's lifetime. On one hand, religion penetrated all phases of life. The atmosphere was
saturated with religious thought. On the other hand, the
Popes lived in "Babylonian captivity" in Avignon. Reform-
ist tendencies alarmed the pious, and the Great Schism
considerably weakened the Church toward the end of the
century. In such a period of strain, any novelty is apt to
be regarded with suspicion. The religious writers of the
time who condemned new features of the liturgy and of the
religious realm as a whole seemed concerned not merely
about the piety, but also about the steady increase, of the
innovations. The author of a treatise *De Reformatione*,
Pierre d'Ailly, who shortly after Machaut's death became
chancellor of the University and of the Notre Dame cathedral in Paris, denounced the growing number of churches,
saints, and holidays. He warned against the multitude of
images and paintings, the overloading of the service. He
protested against the introduction of new hymns and
prayers. What seemed to alarm him was not so much the
idea of novelty as the evil of superfluity.[24]

The constant blending of holy and profane thought, so
typical of the fourteenth century, results in the danger of
reducing any spiritual situation to a profane commonplace.
Complaints about the behavior of church choirs multiply.
In 1330, when Machaut was a young impressionable man,

Bishop Grandison of Exeter decries offenses committed in the cathedral: "Those who stand at the upper stalls in the choir and have lights within their reach at mattins, knowingly and purposely throw drippings or snuffings from the candles upon the heads or the hair of such as stand at the lower stalls, with the purpose of exciting laughter and perhaps of generating discord." He goes on: "Whereas some ministers do sometimes (and, as we grieve to say, too often) commit plain faults in singing or reading incorrectly, then others who know better (and who should rather have compassion on the ignorant and bewail the defects of their brethren) break out, in the hearing of many, into vulgar words of imprecation and derision." We read of a special devil, Tutivillus, whose duty it was to collect carelessly dropped notes and syllables in a large sack.[11]

The strongest blast against the new style of composition, against the *ars nova*, of which Machaut was an ingenious exponent, came from the Papal palace itself. In Provence, a short geographic distance from Machaut, Pope John XXII in 1324-5 issued a strong bull against the modern polyphonic compositions. To what extent Machaut, himself a canon of the Church, deliberately bowed to the Pope's admonition when composing his Mass a few decades later, the detailed discussion of the Mass in a later chapter will attempt to elucidate. He did not altogether sacrifice the complicated rhythms, the fast notes, the peculiar breaking up of a melody among two voices (*hoqueting*, as it was called), and the setting of a liturgical text for four independent voices. But he was impressed, perhaps coerced, by the severe tone of the bull, which we now quote at length:

"Certain disciples of the new school, much concerned with measured rhythms, write in new notes, preferring to devise methods of their own rather than to continue singing in the old way. The music therefore of the divine offices is now performed with semibreves and minims, and with these notes of small value every composition is pestered. Moreover, they truncate the melodies with hoquets, they lubricate them with counterpoints (*discantibus*), and sometimes they even stuff them with upper parts (*triplis et motetis*) made out of secular songs. So that often they must be losing sight of the fundamental sources of our melodies in the Antiphoner and Gradual, and may thus forget what that is upon which their superstructure is raised. They may become entirely ignorant concerning the ecclesiastical Tones, which they already no longer distinguish, and the limits of which they even confound, since, in the multitude of their notes, the modest risings and temperate descents of the plainsong, by which the scales themselves are to be known one from another, must be entirely obscured. Their voices are incessantly running to and fro, intoxicating the ear, not soothing it, while the men themselves endeavour to convey by their gestures the sentiment of the music which they utter. As a consequence of all this, devotion, the true end of worship, is little thought of, and wantonness, which ought to be eschewed, increases. Thus, it was not without good reason that Boethius said: 'A person who is intrinsically sensuous will delight in hearing these indecent melodies, and one who listens to them frequently will be weakened thereby and lose his virility of soul.'

"This state of things, hitherto the common one, we and our brethren have regarded as standing in need of correction; and we now hasten therefore to banish those methods, nay rather to cast them entirely away, and to put them to flight more effectually than heretofore, far from the house of God. Wherefore, having taken counsel with our brethren, we straitly command that no one henceforward shall think himself at liberty to attempt those methods, or methods like them, in the aforesaid Offices, and especially in the canonical Hours, or in the solemn celebrations of the Mass.

"And if any be disobedient, let him, on the authority of this Canon, be punished by a suspension from office of eight days; either by the Ordinary of the diocese in which the forbidden things are done or by his deputies in places not exempt from episcopal authority, or, in places which are exempt, by such of their offices as are usually considered responsible for the correction of irregularities and excesses, and such like matters.

"Yet, for all this, it is not our intention to forbid, occasionally—and especially upon feast days or in the solemn celebrations of the Mass and in the aforesaid divine offices— the use of some consonances, for example the octave, fifth, and fourth, which heighten the beauty of the melody; such intervals therefore may be sung above the simple ecclesiastical Chant, yet so that the integrity of the Chant itself may remain intact, and that nothing in the authoritative music be changed. Used in such sort the consonances would much more than by any other method both soothe the hearer and arouse his devotion, and also would not destroy religious feeling in the minds of the singers."[47]

This is the setting in which Guillaume de Machaut in the middle of the fourteenth century composed six movements of the Ordinary of the Mass in a coherent polyphonic structure—the first composer, as far as we know, ever to do so.

II. Problems of a Religious Composer

THE composition of the Mass presented Machaut with various problems, which it is now our task to investigate. The isolated character of the Mass among Machaut's compositions is only one difficulty among many. In order to sympathize with his position psychologically rather than historically, a transfer of our investigation into the contemporary scene appears justifiable. We may gain a better insight into Machaut after answering the more general question: what are the limitations surrounding a composer in the middle of the twentieth century who has been inspired or commissioned to write a Mass for a Roman Catholic service?

Popular opinion holds that the contemporary composer, more than any of his predecessors in history, is free to choose his manner of expression. He, unlike composers of earlier generations, is not bound by the specific style of his period. Scholarly research has opened to him the musical treasures, and has familiarized him with the musical thoughts, of past centuries and distant countries to such an extent as to liberate him from the narrow restrictions of his immediate surroundings. Whereas Josquin des Prez around the year 1500 or Beethoven around the year 1800 did not have to be concerned with the problem of style beyond studying the works of their respective teachers and illustrious contemporaries and developing their own drives from there on as from a generally accepted and comprehensible starting point, a composer around 1950 appears to be distracted by a multitude of available techniques. The teachers at his disposal are all composers throughout history, and his colleagues, even the best, are normally considered problematic in terms of expression or communication.

This popular opinion, persuasive as it sounds, obscures various pitfalls. It implies a negation of the principle that art cannot exist without limitation. The freedom described becomes less and less discernible from anarchy. The reverence for technique and for accumulated information about technique soon leads to the sacrifice of human values.

But if these problems are common today to the composers of all types of music, what are the additional difficulties of the composer dedicated to a specific task, such as writing a Mass?

He is bound by a text and he is bound by a purpose.

The bondage to the text he shares with the composers of all vocal music. The problem is not so obvious as it appears on the surface. We are used to making certain concessions to a text that is to be set to music. We expect, for instance, the rhythm of the words to determine the rhythm of the music.

The phrase "Christe eleison" carries an accent on the first and fourth syllables, the second, third, and fifth syllables being decidedly weaker when properly pronounced. Can a composer do anything else but conform when placing notes above these words? Moreover, the two words contain an emotional message, which can be brought out by expressive scanning. "Christe eleison," Christ have mercy on us—the tension flows toward the middle of the word "eleison," have mercy. Thus we would voice the prayer, the steepness and amplitude of the curve increasing with the emotional charge of the moment. Thus Beethoven, for instance, has set the phrase in his *Missa Solemnis*.

The text also determines another kind of expression which may be called a "symbolic" one. An old tradition, which bloomed to full strength in the musical Baroque period around 1700, links certain significant words and phrases to ever more standardized musical devices by intellectual rather than musical associations. At the word "ascendit," an ascending figure becomes obligatory; at the word "descendit," a descending one. The Credo of the early C-minor Mass by Mozart (K. 139) affords as good an example as any. The word "altissimus" appropriates a high pitch and "mortuos" affects a whisper.

Besides influencing the rhythm and expression of isolated moments, the text also sets a frame for the composition as a whole. Does a composer have any choice regarding the scope of a composition once the text is given? Can he make a long score out of a short text? A short score out of a long text? Can he ignore in his musical setting certain literary correspondences, such as the typical parallelisms in a psalm verse ("The Lord is my light and my salvation; whom shall I fear? The Lord is the refuge of my life; of whom shall I be afraid?") or the return of the exclamation "Kyrie eleison" after the intermediate "Christe eleison"?

Notwithstanding all these strong arguments for the supremacy of the words that give substance to a vocal composition, the questions raised in the last paragraph can be answered in the affirmative. To sympathize with the unfolding possibilities, we need only free ourselves from the ascendancy of literary thinking, which is prevalent in our time. Language has its laws, and so has music. Whatever points of contact and analogies exist between the poetic and the musical arts, one must never forget the essential areas of intrinsic difference and independence. Each art has its own grammar and syntax, its own powers and own limitations. There is no natural basis for claiming the sovereignty of one art over another. The question is one of co-ordination within a common area. Depending on one's philosophical convictions, one may, of course, declare oneself for a favorite. Plato rated music above all other arts for reasons that prompted Kant to place it at the bottom. Goethe did not respond to Schubert's settings of his poems, because the music did not co-ordinate with the words. Bach and Verdi, on the other hand, adhered throughout their creative lives to poetry of doubtful literary qualities, precisely in order to remain unhampered in the execution of their purely musical plans.

The relegation of language to a subservient role is unpalatable to a modern mind reared in a rational tradition. But the modern mind and the rational tradition are only isolated samples of many kinds of possible minds and possible traditions. The fourteenth century, for instance, of which Machaut is a most expressive part, is bound by aesthetic considerations that differ significantly from those generally representative of the twentieth century. The illustrations from the realms of rhythm, expression, and structure, given before to demonstrate the bondage of the music to the text, can easily be matched by examples from Machaut's works (as well as from many other sources) which refute the alleged obligation.

In the phrase "Christe eleison," according to the most likely disposition of the text in Machaut's famous Mass, the first syllable is set to one single musical note, filling one unit of measured time, whereas the unaccented second syllable is extended to last nineteen times as long in the two upper voices and sixteen and eighteen times as long, respectively, in the two other voices. The first note, moreover, occupies an upbeat position in the over-all rhythmic structure of the whole movement.[19] Even with full recognition of the fact that Latin—far more than English—did not identify long with accented syllables and often lengthened the sound of a weak vowel (oratorical pronunciation of the Latin words "hómines" and "bónae" and of the English words "prélūde" and "ténfōld" will illustrate the point), a nineteen-to-one relationship can be justified only by one circumstance: the fourteenth-century composer does not care to have the scanning of the text control the rhythm of his music. This attitude does not indicate that he is less sensitive than a twentieth-century composer, or less skilled or less sophisticated. He is simply concerned with other problems. He focuses his artistic attention on matters which are neither better nor worse than those interesting a composer of a later period. They are merely different.

Nor do the devices that sound expressive to us necessarily touch an audience brought up to listen for other qualities in a composition. We in the twentieth century have so deeply imbibed the Romantic tradition that we take certain standards as generally valid. Does the composition sound well? Does it affect our emotions of the moment? These questions that assume such great importance today were barely raised at other times. The wallowing in sound for expressive reasons is a recent characteristic. Composers for centuries before and after Machaut hardly cared whether a work was sung or played, fiddled or blown, or performed by individuals or larger ensembles. Similarly, the question of whether a composition was "moving" did not occupy the forefront of attention. This statement must not be misconstrued. People of all times and places have experienced emotional responses to music. But the emphasis on the one or the other quality of a composition has shifted. Machaut's Mass certainly affected his contemporaries who heard it. Many factors came into play. Among the least important was the expressive treatment for emotional reasons of an individual phrase like "eleison." In the Christe section—we follow the most likely disposition of the text—three of the four voices give least emphasis to the middle syllable of the word "eleison," which (one remembers the Beethoven example) should deserve most by other standards. Only the Gregorian tenor voice, at this spot the lowest of the four, follows the inclination of the text. To be more specific, the lively top voice of the triplum allots three beats (on four notes) to the syllable *e-*; one beat (on two notes) to the critical syllable *-lei-*; and six beats (on one note) to the final syllable *-son*. In the second voice, the motetus, the relation is four beats (on two notes), one beat (on one note), and six beats (on one note). Machaut knew the rules of Latin diction as well as we do. The expressive possibilities of the word "eleison" interested him little compared to problems of line, rhythm, structure, and concordant organization.

Symbolism in Machaut's music has been mentioned as characteristic of the general attitude of his century. What interests us at this point is the direct symbolic translation of certain words into musical sounds. In vain we expect a high-pitched exclamation on the word "altissimus." We detect some descending lines on the word "descendit," only to hear very similar lines a few sentences later on the antonym "ascendit." There is, on the other hand, an awesome cessation of independent movement and rhythmic liveliness among the voices at both instances when "Jesu Christe" is directly invoked in the Gloria.

Machaut is not the only composer to venture a musical correction of certain literary disparities among the portions of the Mass. The Kyrie contains six words three times repeated, a total of eighteen words. The Gloria contains eighty-four words, and the Credo one hundred and sixty-three. Mozart, writing four centuries later than Machaut, also creates musical structures that follow their own rather than purely textual limitations. The brief portions are fully developed by letting each syllable be sounded across many notes. This kind of writing has been called melismatic. The lengthy portions, on the other hand, are quickly recited by placing each syllable on a new note. This kind of writing has been called syllabic. The Credo of the Machaut Mass, for example, passes much more quickly than the Kyrie because of consistent syllabic treatment of the former and melismatic treatment of the latter.

Nor is the ternary organization of the text "Kyrie eleison—Christe eleison—Kyrie eleison" mirrored by Machaut's musical setting. This statement refers not merely to the obvious difference between the supplied Gregorian melodies which Machaut's tenor obeys. In this respect he had no choice. But throughout the recapitulation of the Kyrie section one gains the feeling that the music is striving for deliberate independence from the strict symmetry of the text. The rhythmic incisions introduce fresh principles of organization. The whole structure becomes more intense by being first tightly compressed in time and then forcefully expanded. Compared to the analogous situation in the opening Kyrie exclamation, shorter note values are introduced, the nervousness of which becomes all the more agitated by frequent pauses irregularly distributed. The two top voices, which had initially supported each other, now repeatedly break up the melody among themselves in the peculiar manner called hoqueting. It would have been easy for Machaut to assimilate if not the exact notes, at any rate the general attitudes, of the two Kyrie sections. But the musician in him refused in this instance to yield to the temptation offered by the words.

Thus far we have discussed the problems that a given text, such as that of the Mass, may impose upon a composer. We now turn to the more particular difficulties of a composer bound by a purpose.

We may receive a three-dimensional view of the sacred purpose of a religious composer by first looking at his antipode: the composer of popular dance music. He, too, writes for a clearly defined purpose. What motivates him is not so much the urge to create and organize as the intention to amuse and be accepted. In carrying out this intention, he is bound by unwritten laws of his trade, which are so strong that he has little chance of success if he does not abide by them. The facts concerning the writing of popular music have been thoroughly analyzed by a modern scholar. "The whole structure of popular music is standardized, even where the attempt is made to circumvent standardization. Standardization extends from the most general features to the most specific ones. Best known is the rule that the chorus consists of thirty-two bars and that the range is limited to one octave and one note. The general types of hits are also standardized: not only the dance types, the rigidity of whose pattern is understood, but also the 'characters' such as mother songs, home songs, nonsense or 'novelty' songs, pseudo-nursery rhymes, laments for a lost girl. Most

important of all, the harmonic cornerstones of each hit—
the beginning and the end of each part—must beat out the
standard scheme. This scheme emphasizes the most primitive harmonic facts no matter what has harmonically inter-
vened. Complications have no consequences. This inexor-
able device guarantees that regardless of what aberrations
occur, the hit will lead back to the same familiar experience,
and nothing fundamentally novel will be introduced."[1]
This kind of standardization aims at standard reactions.

A sociologist is needed to isolate and describe the principles that control—below the surface, as it were—the
twentieth-century composer intent on writing a popular
dance tune. The principles that govern the composer of
Roman Catholic church music are openly and unambigu-
ously laid down by the Vatican. In November 1903, Pope
Pius X published an edict regarding music in the divine
liturgy. The formula "Motu Proprio" ("by his own motion," i.e., the Pope's) stands at the head of many documents
in which the Pope either justifies the extraordinary character of a concession or wishes to produce definite juridical
effects. The two Latin words have, in common practice,
given the name to the entire edict on music.[37]

A short introduction demands the most scrupulous ob-
servance of the instruction contained in the *Motu Proprio*,
which is to be interpreted as the juridical code of sacred
music. The introduction also gives as an immediate reason
for the publication the deplorable quality of music often
heard in churches. There are compositions that disturb and
lessen the devotion of the faithful. They give cause for dis-

taste or scandal and directly offend the decorum of the sacred functions. The abuse in the matter of sacred music is unworthy of the House of Prayer and of God's Majesty. One finds a constant tending to stray from the correct norm set up by the purpose for which art is admitted to the service of worship. The abuse is common and difficult to eradicate, either because of the fluctuating and variable nature of music, or because of the successive shifts in taste and custom throughout the course of time, or because of the evil influence of profane and theatrical art on sacred art, or because of the pleasure directly produced by music, which is not always kept within just bounds, or finally because of the many prejudices that so easily arise in this matter and are so stubbornly held even among responsible and pious persons.

The general principles of sacred music are concisely formulated in the first two paragraphs of the edict proper, of which the subsequent twenty-seven paragraphs provide a detailed elaboration.

The principal function of sacred music is to adorn the liturgical text. A suitable melody will add greater efficacy to the text itself. By this means the faithful will be more easily moved to devotion and better disposed to receive the fruits of grace.

The implications of this opening paragraph are of utmost importance. It decides in an authoritative manner among various aesthetic possibilities. Music is subservient to the text, just as the text in turn is subservient to the solemn liturgy. Music is a means to a clearly defined end. The liturgy sanctifies the faithful, and music can contribute to this general purpose. Music is acceptable if it enhances the effect of the sacred text. This is the criterion. Music is not acceptable if it is written or played for its own sake. The autonomous laws of music as an art have to yield to those of the liturgy.

Subservience to the text is not the only restriction. Church music must also make the listener disposed to be receptive rather than critical.

What qualities must a composition possess to meet these conditions? The second paragraph of the *Motu Proprio* names three essentials: church music must be holy, good, and universal.

These three qualities deserve thought and care. The musician can objectively produce and recognize such characteristics as high and low, fast and slow, loud and soft, consonant and dissonant; but how can he know what tone combination renders a composition holy?

The initial definition of the *Motu Proprio* approaches the question from the negative side. A composition is holy when it excludes all profanity. *Definitio ne sit negans,* but Satan is more easily described than God, and profanity more easily than holiness. The edict gives various examples. *Profane* may refer to "the theatrical style that was in greatest vogue during the last century, especially in Italy. By its very nature this offers the greatest opposition to . . . good sacred music. Besides the intrinsic structure, the rhythm and so-called 'conventionalism' of this style correspond badly to the requirements of true liturgical music."[37]

Profane may refer to the manner in which music is presented by the performer. Any language other than Latin can give rise to worldly associations and is therefore forbidden in the solemn liturgical functions. The text must be sung as it stands in the holy books, without alteration or inversion of words, without undue repetition, without breaking syllables, and always in a way intelligible to the faithful who listen. The singers in church have a liturgical function. Hence, women, being incapable of such a function, cannot profane the choir by their presence. Nor must the solo voice, although it is not entirely excluded, ever predominate; for any display of human vanity suggests a concert hall rather than a holy place of worship. As a matter of fact, only men of known piety and modest demeanor are to be admitted to form part of the choir, hiding their earthly individualities behind ecclesiastical garb and surplice and architectural gratings.

All these restrictions may not explain the inherent essence of holy music but they isolate various dangers of profanation. The condition that music serve the text cannot be met if there is no text, in short, if the music is not vocal. Instruments are tools of a mundane endeavor. They can be admitted to the church only within due bounds and with proper safeguards, and never without the special permission of the Ordinary. Apparently the pianoforte and noisy or frivolous percussion instruments know no bounds and cannot be checked by safeguards, for they remain excluded from the church at all times. So are bands, which receive the dispensation to accompany pious singers taking

part in a procession outside the church. Only the organ is allowed in the church without special permission. But it must simply sustain and never oppress the vocal chant, be it by the force of sound, or the length of preludes, or the independence of interrupting intermezzo pieces.

Modern science classifies instruments according to the source of tone production. The vibration causing sound may be set off by a string, an air column, a membrane, the material of the instrument itself, or an electric current. Accordingly, we distinguish between stringed instruments, wind instruments, percussion instruments, and the recently developed electrical instruments. The Baroque age classified instruments with less regard to science than to the performance practice of the period. The parts of an orchestration were usually distinguished not so much by timbre as by pitch. A treatise on instruments, written and published in the early seventeenth century by Michael Praetorius, groups the existing instruments according to range and function. A trumpet and a violin, for instance, each can play a high melody. They are therefore jointly contrasted to such instruments as a bass viol, which traces the lowest line of the score, or a lute and organ, which can realize the inherent harmonies of a composition by improvising chords. The classification of the *Motu Proprio* may be called neither scientific nor practical but ethical. The organ is a "good" instrument, the pianoforte a "bad" one. A violin is "better" than a clarinet, and a snare drum is "worse" than either. The governing principle, one readily surmises, is the degree of affinity to the human voice. The idea of a hierarchy among

instruments is representative of the general philosophy of the Roman Catholic Church, but a grouping of instruments by ethical standards was known to the Greeks. The contemporaries of Plato set the holiness of stringed instruments against the profanity of wind instruments. The former were endemic in Greece, invented by Apollo and consecrated to him. Whether his bow first indicated the possibility of converting a weapon into a musical tool ("Fearfully came the clang of the bent bow's shivering silver") or whether it was the legendary turtle that he found on the seashore, the stringed lyre was heard in the temple of the god and was sanctified by the association. Wind instruments, on the other hand, were an exotic importation from barbaric Asia. Wild fauns and satyrs blew their pipes in accompaniment to the orgiastic rites of Dionysus. The god of wine and lust listened to the double-reeded *aulos,* and the audiences at the theaters and athletic games shared his frenetic thrill.

The scientific and practical classifications of instruments can be justified on purely musical grounds. From where do instruments derive their ethical significance? Will the organ retain its sacred sound to ears more and more accustomed to hearing it in a movie theater or night club? The trumpet is used as a military instrument in Beethoven's *Missa Solemnis,* threatening the peace invoked by the Agnus Dei. But in Bach's Mass, it signals the glory of the Lord. Is the mellow dignity of the saxophone outlawed only because of its unholy association with jazz bands?

The holiness of music permitted in church has been defined by the *Motu Proprio* as that quality that excludes all

profanity not only from the score but also from the manner
of performance. The given examples of profanity seem to
come from apparently unrelated realms. But theatrical style,
pronounced rhythm, conventionalism, secular language, im-
provisation, solo performance, exhibitionism, supremacy of
instrumental over vocal expression, and prevalence of noisy
percussion instruments—these characteristics reveal a common root to the critical musician. Although the *Motu Proprio* does not single out or even name the constitutional
antagonist of church music, we recognize dance music as
the carrier of all the profane qualities listed before and as
worthy of our special attention.

There is no doubt that the dance, at the opposite pole
and rivaling the dynamic force of spirituality, has produced
original musical qualities of the first order. To the extent
that instrumental compositions are not transcriptions of
vocal models, they must be credited to the generating power
of the dance. The development of instrumental music in
the Renaissance bears witness to this fact. The conventionalism of most musical dance forms—be they the alternation
of duple and triple rhythms in the sixteenth century or of
verse and refrain in the twentieth—has satisfied the dancers
of all centuries and civilizations. Precisely this conventionalism has also made possible improvised and individualized
expression—the medieval fiddler and the swing clarinetist
are close cousins.

One of the reasons for our relatively limited knowledge
of the influence of dance music stems directly from the opposition of the Church. Most early histories were written by

men who either belonged to the Church, or who were inspired by it, or who attested by their mere literacy their
allegiance to the spiritual rather than the vulgar world. In
any case, their prejudice against dance music appears ex-
cusable, and they either condemn or ignore it in favor of
the sacred vocal style.

We learn as much from the silence of some authors as
from the outspokenness of others. The use of dance music
and instruments was repugnant to the primitive Christians;
and this aversion may be ascribed to their reaction against
the Jews and their enmity to the Greeks. The Mosaic law had
encouraged the oriental custom of a loud and tumultuous
worship. When David first attempted to bring the ark of
God to Jerusalem, he placed it in a new cart while he "and
all Israel played before God with all their might, with songs
and harps and lyres and tambourines and cymbals and
trumpets" (I Chron. 13:8). When he later succeeded, the
return of the ark to Jerusalem was accompanied "with
shouting and with the sound of the cornet and trumpets
and cymbals sounding aloud, with lyres and harps" (I Chron.
15:28). At the dedication of the temple by King Solo-
mon, David's son, "the Levites who were singers, all of
them, Asaph, Heman, Jeduthun, their sons, and their kins-
men, clothed in fine linen, with cymbals, lyres, and harps,
stood at the east side of the altar and with them a hundred
and twenty priests blowing upon trumpets. Now when the
trumpeters and singers joined in unison to make a great
volume of sound in praising and thanking the Lord and
when they raised a sound with trumpets and with cymbals

and with instruments of song, and when they praised the Lord . . . then the house was filled with a cloud" (II Chron. 5:12-13).

The condemnation of such practices was a conscious reaction of the Church against Jewish and heathenish customs. St. Chrysostom, in the fourth century after Christ, advocates the expulsion of instrumental and the reign of vocal music by decrying the lifeless strings of David's harp as compared to the living strings of a singing congregation. An edict issued around the year 370 prohibits religious worship by soulless instruments and by stamping and dancing; after the elimination of such childish manifestations, only pure singing shall remain. At the same time, St. Athanasius emphatically declares himself against the oriental custom of clapping and dancing to the tune of hymns. From the urgency of these and similar proscriptions one fact emerges with certainty: congregations were clapping and dancing. The influence of dance and instrumental music was strong and it was considered pernicious. To the Anglo-Saxon Bishop Aldhelm, who died in 709, the organ still appears as a tool of oriental, heathenish enticement; and only the authority of Charlemagne one century later installs it in the place of dignity in which it has been held until today.[22] The origin of the prejudice against instruments remains evident to the critical wisdom of all centuries. More than one thousand years after Christianity split from Judaism, St. Thomas Aquinas states that the Church does not use instruments for fear of seeming to imitate the Jews.[2]

An inimical force can be conquered in two ways, by being

surmounted or by being absorbed. The Church used both in meeting the threat of profanation by dance music. While saints and preachers, bulls and letters, attempted to overcome force by force, religious composers subtly practiced, and discerning bishops tolerated, the transformation of popular dance tunes into compositions of worship. The kind of transformation has varied with musical style but the general practice has been familiar to each. Roman Catholic, and later Protestant, composers have artfully availed themselves of secular melodies in favor with the crowd by introducing them into musical scores of the service. The profane root might not be openly declared but it remains audible to the attentive and gratified ear in characteristics of a fragmentary or entire melody structure; in the pronounced line of one of the voices in a polyphonic motet; in the melodic substance of a whole Mass; or in the straightforward tune of a sacred hymn. Music history is full of examples. A few selected illustrations will testify to the psychological success of this refined practice.

There is evidence that Gregorian chant, which was codified around the year 600, contains elements not only of sacred Jewish and Greek music to which Rome fell heir, but also of popular local Italian music of the day. Arius, now known as a heretic, deliberately introduced into the public service the kind of music that might impress his particular doctrine on the popular ear. He collected songs of sailors, millers, and travelers and set them to liturgical texts. The ignorant were beguiled by the familiar sweetness of his music. Arian singers, it is reported, paraded the streets of

Constantinople by night, spreading their doctrine on the wings of popular songs, until Chrysostom arrayed against them a band of orthodox choristers.[18]

Many dance tunes of the Renaissance have been better preserved by the superior Mass in which they were incorporated than by their own fleeting lineage. The tune "L'homme armé" ("The armed man"), for instance, was a popular French folk song of the fifteenth century. Antoine Busnois, the celebrated pupil of Ockeghem and chapel-singer to Charles the Bold of Burgundy, made a polyphonic art song of it. The melody (which begins somewhat like the last Brahms-Haydn variation) quickly proved its usability for other than secular purposes. We know today of more than thirty Masses based on this melody. The best composers were attracted to it: Dufay, Busnois, Ockeghem, Josquin des Prez, Senfl, Palestrina, and Carissimi. (The German composer Johann Nepomuk David composed a "Fantasia super L'homme armé" for organ in 1930.) The tune was used in its entirety, broken up into shorter motifs, augmented, or diminished; and eventually it became so absorbed by the polyphonic structure as to lose its identity. The ingenious approach of a modern scholar, Dragan Plamenac, was necessary to find and reconstruct the original text in 1925. The apprehension of the Church could not stop the practice of utilizing a good worldly tune for a good religious purpose. When the Council of Trent forbade the composition of Masses on secular *cantus firmi*, composers dropped the habit of openly naming a Mass after the tune on which it was built, *Missa L'homme armé*. But they did not drop the tune itself. Palestrina's *Missa quarta* of 1582 is based on "L'homme armé." Occasionally the title *Missa sine nomine* (Mass without a name) hides the identity but not the liveliness of the secular source. Today, when most listeners no longer have ready associations with the profane original, the ban on these old Masses could be lifted without giving offense.

The *cantus firmus*, subtly imbedded in a score, bears witness to an ingenious technique. But little craft was applied in the transformation of popular tunes into hymns, that prevailed in the periods of the Reformation and Counter Reformation. Students used to sing a ditty when leaving their university town at the end of a term; substitution of one word changed "Innsbruck, I now must leave thee" to "O world, I now must leave thee," and religion gained new adherents by the adoption of a melody. A popular tune, "Mein mut ist mir betrübet gar" ("My heart is very sad") opens a song collection written down by a Nürnberg citizen around 1450. The composer Hans Leo Hasler, of the same town, used the melody in a small piece for chorus, which was widely sung around 1600 as a lover's lament to the words "Mein G'müt ist mir verwirret" ("My heart is all confused"). For this secular "hit," the Protestant poet Paul Gerhardt found a new text by freely translating St. Bernard's mystical "Salve caput cruentatum" into "O Haupt, voll Blut und Wunden" ("O head, full of blood and wounds"). And in this version one hears it today, as the often recurring and deeply moving chorale in Bach's *Passion According to St. Matthew.*

Is a modern congregation aware of the fact that "Onward, Christian Soldiers" is a march, Handel's "And the Glory of the Lord" a minuet, "Rock of Ages" a pastorale, and "Oh, that will be Glory for me" a waltz? The conquest of popular music by the Church is by no means historically dated, as two examples of recent years demonstrate. One is taken from fiction, if the sensitive insight of a poet deserves to be called fictitious. In an early chapter of *The Grapes of Wrath*, John Steinbeck introduces the preacher Jim Casy. Sitting under a tree, Jim Casy "was whistling solemnly the tune of 'Yes, Sir, That's My Baby.' His extended foot swung slowly up and down in the tempo. It was not dance tempo. He stopped whistling and sang in an easy thin tenor:

'Yes, sir, that's my Saviour,
Je-sus is my Saviour,
Je-sus is my Saviour now.
On the level
'S not the devil,
Jesus is my Saviour now!' "*

In October 1944, the Jesuit magazine *The Queen's Work* called attention to a new Mass composed by a young nun of San Antonio.[26] The Mass is based on folk tunes of the American Negro; but the noted Catholic editor of the magazine, Father Daniel Lord, thinks that it should satisfy the high standards of canonical law and that Pope Pius X himself, the sainted author of the *Motu Proprio,* "would have approved most enthusiastically of this transference of

* Viking Press.

a great series of musical themes to the greatest of musical purposes." The expert professional hand of Sister Mary Elaine, the composer, has knitted into each section of the Mass the theme of a well-known spiritual. The invocation of the Kyrie is expressed by "Nobody Knows de Trouble I've Seen"; the glory of the next section by "Go Down, Moses." The Credo is announced by "Blow Your Trumpet, Gabriel." The sections of the Sanctus and Benedictus are carried by the tunes of "Goin' Home" and "Swing Low, Sweet Chariot." The closing prayer of the Agnus Dei follows the melody of "Deep River."

Using the distinctions of the *Motu Proprio* as a starting point, we have tried to describe the cleavage of holy and profane music. A historian of the civilization and period to which Machaut belonged has applied his knowledge and sensitivity to a speculation on the existence and development of this dualism. Johan Huizinga's words might summarize our long inquiry into the qualities of holiness and profanity in art.[24] "Toward the end of the Middle Ages the choice lay between God and the world: total denouncing of the glamour and beauty of earthly life or eager grasping at the peril of one's soul. The beauty of the world doubled its lure by the implication of sinfulness. Those who wished neither to neglect beauty nor to abandon themselves to the world were forced to ennoble beauty. They could sanctify the whole province of art and literature, where admiration is essential to enjoyment, by placing it in the service of religion. While the delight in color and line inspired the lovers of paintings and miniatures, the holy object of the art works purified the enjoyment from the taint of sin.

"The great change in the attitude toward beauty occurs between the Renaissance and modern times. The turning point lies where art and life begin to separate; where one enjoys art no longer in the middle of life as an integral and noble part of the *joie de vivre* but outside of life as something to be highly revered and attended to in moments of exaltation or of relaxation. The old dualism which parted God and the world has here returned, in another form, in the partition of art and life. Now a line runs through the middle of the pleasures of life. They are henceforth divided in two halves, a lower and a higher one. To the medieval man they were altogether sinful; now they are all permissible, but their ethical evaluation varies with their higher or inferior spirituality.

"The elements that can make life pleasurable have remained the same. Now as then they are: literature, music, fine arts, travel, nature, sport, fashion, social vanity, and sensual intoxication. But the dividing line between high and low shifts. For most modern men it seems to run between nature and sport. For the medieval man it ran, at best, directly below literature. Even the pleasure of reading could be sanctified only by the pursuit of virtue or wisdom; and music and the fine arts were recognized as good only in so far as they could be of service to religion. Pleasure by itself was sinful. The Renaissance, on the other hand, endeavored to find pleasure in all of life. The new partition is the result of a compromise between Renaissance and Puritanism, which characterizes the modern mind. It represents a capitulation on both sides, whereby the one stipulated the salvation of beauty, the other the condemnation of sin. Whoever today were to draw the dividing line between higher and lower pleasures of life according to the dictates of our ethical conscience, would no longer separate art from sensuality, nature from sport, or aspiration from naturalness, but only egotism, falseness, and vanity from purity."

Holiness, one remembers, is only one of three qualities that sacred music must possess, according to the general principles of the *Motu Proprio*. We still have to inquire into the problems facing the religious composer concerned with goodness of form and with universality, the other two qualities. Whereas holiness appears to be the exclusive property of church music, goodness of form, and, to a certain extent, universality are expected to characterize all manifestations of composition. Hence, the remainder of our inquiry will be focused on those aspects of the latter two conditions that are peculiar to the sanctifying and edifying purpose of religion.

Goodness of form, in particular, can hardly be discussed outside the frame of a given philosophical system. The intrinsic merits of a work of art constitute the central question of aesthetics, and the answer depends on the emphasis one is inclined to lend to such concepts as expression, loftiness of thought, intention, unity, cohesion, appropriateness of devices, amusement, or instruction.

The *Motu Proprio* rather justifies than explains the quality of goodness. Sacred music must be true art, "for otherwise it is not possible for it to have that effect on listeners which the Church intends to achieve in admitting the art of music into her liturgy."[37] Here lies the meeting point with the pure musician. His standards are accepted if he, in turn, bows to the superior function of the solemn liturgy. Truth and goodness in art are not peculiar to any special period or style. "The Church has always recognized and favored the progress of the arts, admitting to the service of worship everything good and beautiful that genius has been able to discover throughout the centuries—always however with due regard for liturgical laws. Consequently, modern music is also admitted in church, as it also offers compositions of such goodness, seriousness, and gravity that they are not at all unworthy of liturgical functions."[37] Any area of compromise admits most readily of controversy. Who is to decide whether a composition is "good"? History has conveniently performed the service of a judge. The survival or disappearance of compositions written centuries ago may be accepted as a fair measurement of their inherent value. It is not likely that there has existed a great composer of the stature of Machaut, Ockeghem, or Josquin des Prez without our knowing about him today. The occasional survival of an inferior score testifies only to a human tolerance which gives the benefit of the doubt to the result of any effort before condemning it. But in the case of contemporary music, history leaves the judicial seat vacant for anyone to occupy; and the quickest and loudest usurpers are seldom the best. Without the security of judgment derived from the lapse of centuries, one is reduced to relying on one's own process of sifting. Those who lack critical standards of their own and mistrust the critical methods of others may turn for guidance to the St. Gregory Societies in various countries, which pass on the suitability of music for liturgical use. Admonished by Pope Pius XII, the Societies maintain a strict watch against the intrusion of bizarre, unusual effects.[36]

The religious composer attentive to goodness of form must heed certain minor restrictions imposed by the subordination of the score to the text of the liturgy. He may not tamper with the order of the prescribed texts, nor change them, nor omit them entirely or even only in part. He must preserve the unity of each section of the Mass. Hence he is not allowed to parse a long movement into separate pieces, so that each of these pieces would form a complete composition. He must preserve the traditional form of hymns of the Church; thus he is "not allowed to compose, for instance, a *Tantum Ergo* in such a way that the first strophe would present a romanza, a cavatina, an adagio, and the *Genitori* an allegro."[37] The antiphons of Vespers must never have the form of a concert melody or the extent of a motet or cantata.

The good religious composer is also restricted by his submission to the priest, whom he is not permitted to keep waiting at the altar because of the singing, longer than is fitting to the liturgical ceremony. The Sanctus, for instance, must be finished before the elevation, and the Gloria and Credo must be relatively short. The earnest composer must beware not to be condemned for the very grave abuse of overshadowing the liturgy by the strength and beauty of the music, "since music is simply a part of the liturgy and its humble handmaid."[37]

This last metaphor, exact to the word, occurs in another famous quotation, and invites a comparison of the two instances. In a letter to his father, on 13 October 1781, Mozart writes: "In an opera, the poetry must be the handmaid of the music." Notwithstanding the difference between a mass and an opera, they share the basic problem of correlating words and music. Can we pit the authority of Mozart against that of the Church? The two statements can exist next to each other if one remembers the intentions they represent. Mozart is a musician. His art determines his life; and other art forms, such as literature, remain ancillary to his own mode of expression. In his operas, the arias and ensembles are basically instrumental forms in which the human voice also acts as an instrument. Mozart's supreme purpose is to write music. The supreme purpose of the solemn liturgy, however, of which sacred music is an integral part, is to give glory to God and to sanctify and edify the faithful. Since the contribution of music is measured by the increase of decorum and splendor of the ecclesiastical ceremonies, it remains apodictically a means toward an end and hence subservient to the liturgical text.

What are the musical characteristics of universality, the third quality sacred music must possess in the highest degree? The *Motu Proprio* implies that universality is the inevitable and spontaneous product of holiness and goodness of form. In the years when the Roman Empire impressed upon Europe a unified idea of culture, the tribes at the remote corners of the Empire may have occasionally succumbed to the taste of the civilized center; and Britons, Spaniards, and Greeks may have found inspiration from hearing and singing melodies that contained elements familiar to each of them. The music was uniformly monophonic: even in a chorus everybody followed the same line. The range of the lines stayed within clearly recognized limits, and the steps from tone to tone approached standardization. We may again reach the point of sharing a common fate and of developing a unified expression, but in the past millennium the idea of universality has lain in abeyance while national prerogatives and idiosyncrasies have triumphed. Can we be expected to derive a direct aesthetic pleasure from the chant of a Tibetan monk? Are we, in turn, entitled to scorn him for not reacting to the intricacies of a Brahms symphony? Still the musical substance of both is based on the same fundamental facts and is thus far universal.

The *Motu Proprio* allows every nation to admit into its ecclesiastical compositions particular characteristics of its own music. Yet these traits of a national idiom must be subordinated to the general character of sacred music in such a way that no one of another nation may receive a bad impression on hearing them. The exclusion of any language except the supranational Latin insures an additional protection.

The Mass on Negro spirituals written by Sister Mary

Elaine comes to mind. Americans, and not only Negroes, respond with considerable pleasure to the rhythm and inflection of "Nobody Knows de Trouble I've Seen." Shall we be able to maintain the claim of the tune for universal appeal before the unresponsive congregation of another continent?

Questions like those raised by our inquiry into the musical characteristics of holiness, goodness of form, and universality are often the subject matter of aesthetic speculations, which however, rarely venture to submit definitive answers. The *Motu Proprio*, probably alone in the literature concerned with artistic values, makes available a precision measuring rod which can be applied to any composition. The exactness of the standard is made possible by the dogma of the Church. "The more closely a composition for church approaches the Gregorian melody in movement, inspiration, and flavor, the more sacred and liturgical it is; and the more it departs from that supreme model, the less worthy it is of the temple."[37] The qualities of holiness, goodness of form, and universality, which Gregorian chant possesses in the highest degree, are also found in an eminent degree in the classical polyphony, especially of the Roman school, which in the sixteenth century reached its highest perfection in the work of Pierluigi da Palestrina. Classical polyphony may be considered quite close to the supreme model of Gregorian chant. If we remember that the Italian opera style of the nineteenth century—the music of Donizetti, Rossini, and Verdi—is singled out by the *Motu Proprio* as offering "the greatest opposition to

Gregorian chant and to classical polyphony," we now discern the exact extension and some notches on our measuring rod. Gregorian chant lies at one end, *Rigoletto* at the other. Palestrina and his school are slightly less "good" than Gregorian chant. Then compositions become gradually "worse" as they admit the influx of conventional rhythms, dance patterns, instrumental forms, vainglorious effects, and theatrical motifs, until the excess of profanity is reached by a combination of these elements in Italian opera of the nineteenth century.

The efficiency of this infallible system of values is readily tested. Bach's Mass in B Minor employs a polyphony which is in certain aspects related to that of Palestrina. But on the whole, concerto features and conventional rhythms prevail; and highly individualized expression alternates with dramatic effect and theatrical orchestration. The conception is basically instrumental, in an exacting manner that distracts the audience as well as the performers from the liturgy. The Mass has been forbidden by the Church for use at a liturgical service. Beethoven's *Missa Solemnis* is even "worse"; for the saving grace of Palestrina reminiscences vanishes under the increased pressure of subjective emotion and virtuosity. Rossini's *Stabat Mater*, except for the words, is hardly distinguishable from the general operatic style of its composer. Verdi's *Ave Maria*, for unaccompanied chorus and in disciplined polyphonic style, may encounter difficulties in church, partly because of an enigmatic scale on which the four strophes are built and partly because of the compelling mundane reputation of the author. But it is well to keep in mind that long portions of the last act of *Otello* approach the Gregorian melody in movement, inspiration, and flavor much more closely than Bach's Sanctus. The recent Mass by Stravinsky, on the other hand, makes many deliberate claims to acceptance. The melodic lines are inspired by Gregorian chant; the scant instrumentation remains subservient to the singers, who in turn seldom forget their respect for the sacred text. The final religious judgment on this work may easily hinge on the interpretation of certain effects, which some may condemn as unusual and bizarre, and which others may accept as serious and worthy.

The precision of the measuring rod, the uniqueness of an absolute system of aesthetics, are sanctioned by the dogma of the Church. The premises on which the system is built are beyond dispute. A similar attempt in the dialectical temporal world may find less sympathy. I know of one contemporary philosopher interested in music who constructed a careful system of aesthetics on the premise that Mozart is the supreme model, and that a composition is the better the closer it approaches his mode of writing. The difficulties of such a system are apparent even to an ardent worshipper of Mozart.

The extraordinary selection of Gregorian chant and of Palestrina from the immeasurable wealth of the totality of music invites a brief consideration of their inherent worth. When Pope Gregory I around the year 600 standardized and codified the kind of music appropriate to the purpose of the Roman liturgy, he wisely drew from sources which were legitimate by tradition and popular by custom. The principle of efficiency along which he steered his many other reforms set a safe course to his concern for the ritual. The melodic substance was derived from the heritage of the Jewish temple, from the kinship with the civilization of Greece and the Orient, and from the forcible contact with the Roman populace.

The amalgamation and purification of these diverse elements into an artistically uniform whole is the achievement of Gregory and his musical assistants. They would hardly have succeeded if the product of their endeavor had not been close to the characteristic musical expression of the day. Gregorian chant is monodic. Only one pure melody is sung at a time, never disturbed by a contrapuntal second voice or even by a simple accompaniment. One must not be confused by the apparent multitude of singers in a choir devoted to Gregorian chant, for all sing the same line. The art of fitting several voices together in one composition so that one melody is attended by other related but independent melodies—this high art of polyphony did not spring into existence until several centuries after the Papal reform and was still in an early, experimental stage when Machaut wrote his Mass almost eight hundred years after Gregory. Today when our total musical culture is fundamentally polyphonic (from the primitively accompanied popular song to the richly orchestrated symphony), and when a single unaccompanied melody is hardly ever heard in performance (a mother's lullaby and a laborer's hum are not meant for outside ears), the style of Gregorian chant

by writing just the right kind of Mass for the Council of Trent has been exploded as a fictitious rationalization of his position. His music, the beauty of which nobody denies, projects neither more control nor more expression than that of a dozen other composers of his day. It is distinctly narrower in scope than Josquin's. The latter died in the same year in which Luther made his famous stand in Worms. Would he have become a Protestant? There is no doubt that Palestrina, born after the outbreak of the great religious conflict, sided with Rome. One suspects that a series of extramusical events, combined with unchallenged merits, catapulted him to the summit where even the nonmusical world could not overlook him.

Such are some of the complex forces that act on a twentieth-century composer writing a Mass for a Roman Catholic service. We have dealt with them extensively because they may help us sympathize more immediately with the problems that faced Guillaume de Machaut in the fourteenth century when he decided to write a Mass. The lapse of six hundred years need not distract us; for both music and the Church claim timeless eternity as their own.

III. The Mass by Machaut

TALKING about a musical composition is like serving a recipe in place of a dinner. In both instances, the verbalization will remain painfully distant from the real event. Our position may be justified by the assumption that a discussion of Machaut's Mass can whet the reader's appetite and lead him to the music itself.

Machaut's Mass is a four-part setting of six portions of the most solemn service of the Roman Catholic rites. One must distinguish between the service itself and those parts that are commonly set to music. The service of the Mass represents the commemoration and mystical re-enactment of the sacrifice of Christ on the cross. The structure of the service is complex and persuasive. Peter Wagner, the musical author of a history of the Mass, gives the following disposition:[44]

1. The celebrant priest and his assistants enter, accompanied by the choir singing the Introit.

2. Confession of sins. The congregation sings the call for mercy, Kyrie Eleison.

3. The celebrant intones the Gloria In Excelsis, which the choir continues.

4. First prayer (collect) and reading from the Bible. The cantor, accompanied by the choir, sings the Gradual and Alleluia (or Tract).

5. The reading from the Bible leads into a sermon. Then the celebrant intones the Credo in Unum Deum.

6. At the altar, the sacred action begins. Bread and wine are blessed and offered. The Offertory is sung.

7. The celebrant renders thanks. The Preface terminates in the Sanctus, sung by the choir.

8. Canon of the Mass. Consecration. After the breaking of the Eucharistic wafer, the Agnus Dei is sung.

9. The Communion accompanies the distribution of the transformed bread.

10. After a final prayer, the congregation is dismissed.

Part of the service is recited and need not concern us here any further. But even among the sung portions, an important differentiation has to be made. Some of them (Introit, Gradual, Alleluia, Offertory, and Communion) vary from day to day. They are called the *proprium missae*, the Proper of the Mass, because the texts and chants change with the proper function of each day and holiday. The Proper is directed mainly toward the altar and the celebrant. It contains most solo numbers, which supply a kind of artistic luster to the service.

There are other sung portions, however, the texts of

which remain the same in every Mass. They are called the *ordinarium missae*, the Ordinary of the Mass, and comprise the Kyrie, Gloria, Credo, Sanctus, Agnus Dei, and the Ite Missa Est. The chants of the Ordinary symbolize the community of all present. They carry the thought and feeling of a general Christian expression without entering into the proper spirit of a specific day. The separation of the individualized Proper from the communal Ordinary is visualized by the physical separation of the celebrant near the altar from the group of singers in the special space of the choir.

One might think that the individualized forms of the Proper have been a temptation to composers through the ages. Actually it is the Ordinary of the Mass that has been responsible for the development of a unified musical structure. In the context of a musical form, the Kyrie, Gloria, Credo, Sanctus, and Agnus Dei express the various types of religious emotion. (The Ite Missa Est has not been composed since Machaut; the factual text leaves it with the chanting priest.) The framing portions, Kyrie and Agnus Dei, correspond to each other by their triple call for mercy. Around the exact central position of the declaration of the creed, Gloria and Sanctus, on either side, sing the praises of the Lord. The *ordinarium missae* thus emerges in wonderful symmetry in the hands of a sensitive composer.[44]

There are also historical and practical reasons for the independent development of the composed Ordinary. The Proper is older. Since its organization was established in the seventh century, it has hardly changed, and its portions have seldom been freshly composed for liturgical use. The Ordinary, on the other hand, remained more flexible, changing from country to country, and escaping official normalization by the ecclesiastic authority throughout the Middle Ages. The resulting liberty attracted composers and protected them against possible conflicts with the liturgy. Moreover, can a composer be blamed for preferring texts that are regularly used and the settings of which can be heard week after week to those texts that are, in most cases, proper only once a year?

Whatever the reason, to a musician the word "Mass" does not connote the entire sacred service but usually only the unified composition of five portions of the Ordinary.

The Kyrie Eleison was originally sung by the whole congregation. The repeated pleas for mercy—reiteration of only two words—established its popularity within a few hundred years after Christ. The number of exclamations was easily adjusted to the needs of the liturgical situation, the people responding to the intonation of the celebrant. The present artistic form began to grow only after the congregation abandoned participation to the ecclesiastical singers in the eleventh century.

The Gloria was originally a hymn, which priests were permitted to chant only on Easter Sunday. Admitted into the Mass at a relatively late date, it has never lost the character of a special festive song, which may be omitted at certain common occasions. The fact that the priest at the altar has to sing the opening phrase as a kind of cue to the choir still conveys the idea that he has the power to include the Gloria or not, although in fact he is following the *ordo* of his diocese.

The most recent portion of the Mass is the Credo, officially accepted in the eleventh century. We read in an old ceremonial that the bishop intoned the Credo whenever he did not want to preach. It was originally a substitute for the sermon. Even today one hears the Credo as a recitation rather than as a song, and composers meet peculiar difficulties reconciling the given wordiness with melodious impulse.

By contrast, the Sanctus is of very great age, inherited by the earliest Christians from the Jewish liturgy. Originally sung by the congregation, it favored freer musical developments, like the Kyrie, only after being taken over by the ecclesiastic choir.

The Agnus Dei was incorporated in the Mass by Pope Sergius I, about one hundred years after Gregory. In the Greek Mass, a rich chant occupies the corresponding place. It is likely that Sergius, a native of Syria, was motivated by a desire to create an analogous portion for the Roman Mass.

Ite Missa Est, composed by Machaut but by nobody after him, means literally translated: "Go, the congregation is dismissed." Nevertheless, this factual statement has given the name to the whole service. Already Ambrosius, in a letter of the year 385, employs the word "missa" as a technical term for the entire eucharistic sacrifice.

The setting of the first portion by Machaut is tripartite, the over-all structure clearly distinguishing between the three sentences of the text: "Kyrie eleison. Christe eleison. Kyrie eleison." These sentences are the sole Greek remnant in the otherwise Latin service. Each sentence has to be said three times. The governing principle of the number three might reflect the glory of the Trinity, in a kind of symbolism which we keep encountering in the course of our investigation. But the nice distinction between *"Lord,* have mercy on us" and *"Christ,* have mercy on us" can be traced to a dualistic interpretation of the incarnation of Christ, which dates back to the fifth century. The patriarch of Constantinople, Nestorius, preached such a discrimination of the humanity of Christ from the divinity of the Lord that he practically made two persons in Christ. St. Cyril of Alexandria rigorously upheld the doctrine of one incarnate person. A Christian synod exclaimed, "May those who divide Christ be divided with the sword," and the dispute affected the lives of many people.[18]

The last Kyrie is neither an exact reiteration of the opening Kyrie nor does it mechanically reproduce its own triplicity. The final repetition begins like its predecessor but soon broadens out to about seven fourths of the original length. Rhythmic agitation increases. Shortly before the end (c^2 in m. 91) the top line works itself up to a high pitch which surpasses all previous accomplishments of the last Kyrie. The effect is singularly climactic. The intention of a "climax" would be risky to impute to a fourteenth-century score if the culmination were not strongly felt by anyone singing or hearing the composition. Moreover, the deliberate and effectual broadening of the final Kyrie "betrays the weakening of purely liturgical considerations and the strengthening of essentially aesthetic concepts" that are significant of Machaut's general attempt to unify the liturgically separate sections of the Ordinary into one musically cohesive art work.[6]

The whole first section of the Kyrie is structurally determined by two principles of composition which were very common to the fourteenth century but which are so removed from modern experience that a circumstantial explanation seems here in order. This movement (as also the "Amen" of the Credo, the Sanctus, Agnus Dei, and Ite Missa Est) is isorhythmic, and it is held together by a *cantus firmus*.

The Greek root *iso* denotes equality, similarity, uniformity, or identity. The term may be familiar from words like isodynamic (having equality of force), isometric (pertaining to equality of measure), or isosceles (having two equal sides). A melody is constructed isorhythmically if a definite grouping of note values, some longer and some shorter, keeps recurring without necessarily retaining the same melodic notes. On a familiar level, the principle of isorhythm can be illustrated by a comparison of the phrase "O say! can you see" with the phrase "by the dawn's early light" or of "God save our gracious Queen!" with "Long live our noble Queen!" The rhythms of the first two phrases of the American anthem, or of the first two lines of the British anthem, are identical, but the tunes are not. Tap the rhythm of "O say! can you see" on a table top; it is exactly repeated by "by the dawn's early light." But sing the first phrase of the anthem and you will not want to repeat the melody for the words of the second phrase. These are examples isolated from the context. You need only continue with "What so proudly we hail'd" or with "God save the Queen!" to realize that your tapped rhythm will no longer fit. The two opening phrases or lines in either example are isorhythmic, but the composition as a whole is not.

In an isorhythmic composition of the late Middle Ages, one or more voices reiterate the same rhythmic group over and over again without, however, necessarily repeating the same tune. The total of one rhythmic group is called a *talea* (French *taille*, incision or section), a technical term used throughout the fourteenth and fifteenth centuries. The tenor of Machaut's first Kyrie, for instance, contains seven *taleae*. This statement means that a definite rhythm recurs, without alteration, seven times to fill the whole movement. Each *talea*, in this case, extends over four measures and is sharply distinguished by a characteristic sequel of longer and shorter notes. But not one of the seven *taleae* repeats the melodic phrase heard in any of the other *taleae*. The rhythms are identical, but the melodies are entirely different.

The term "measure" used in the last paragraph may be called anachronistic by literal pedants but it can also be defended by musicians sensitive to the substance rather than to the name tag of a phenomenon. Today a measure is defined by the total number of beats, be they notes or rests, between two adjacent bar lines. The bar line, fundamentally a device of organization in time, has occasionally

also been interpreted as a device of accentuation by marking
with an accent the note just after it. Whatever its function,
the bar line did not become part of our system of notation
until the Renaissance. The earliest known bar lines appear
in German organ tablatures around 1450. The bar line
and hence the modern concept of "measure" were unknown
to Machaut and his contemporaries in the fourteenth century, but there is no doubt that he was thoroughly familiar
with the idea of a regular measure in time. As a matter
of fact, Machaut's predecessors in the so-called *ars antiqua*,
the old art, of the thirteenth century wrote almost all their
music in rigidly measured groups. These groups were called
"modes" (not to be confused with the melodic modes, or
scales, of antiquity), and the absence of bar lines could not
debilitate their exact "measure" in time nor even the regularly recurring position of the accent. The first rhythmic
mode of the thirteenth century regularly alternated long
and short notes. This rhythmic pattern is more commonly
called trochaic; the word "Christus" is an example. The
second rhythmic mode reverses the order. The rhythmic
pattern of short-long, as in "Deō," is also called iambic.
The third, or dactylic, mode is the one known from the
first movement of Beethoven's Seventh Symphony. The
fourth, or anapaestic, mode, reverses the third (short-long-
longer); sounding somewhat forced, it is rare in music.
The fifth, or spondaic, mode presents a chain of equally
long notes; and the sixth, or tribrachic, mode, of equally
short ones. A combination of a long with a short note adds
up to three time units. The proud name of *tempus per-*

fectum, "perfect meter," professed the superior role of triple rhythm in all medieval music. A bow to the Trinity is implied. In the twentieth century one is apt to consider duple meter the norm, spiritual principles having yielded to the physiological ones of heartbeat and bipedality. This excursion into some intricacies of medieval rhythm would be too long if it were only to prove that the idea if not the term of "measure" existed in the fourteenth century. But it has the additional advantage of increasing our modern sensitivity to certain ageless qualities of Machaut's music. We have described the *talea* of the tenor in the first Kyrie. We can now say that it is in the third rhythmic mode. Machaut's obedience to a somewhat rigid technique of a past century may be symptomatic of his desire to make the Mass acceptable to the Church. In many of his secular compositions he had freed himself from the strict rhythmic modes of the thirteenth century. Now, seemingly heedful of the recent bull issued by Pope John XXII, he ceased "devising rhythmic methods" of his own and deliberately continued "singing in the old way."

The third rhythmic mode is perhaps the most pronounced of all six, by virtue of its strong profile. Therefore a modern ear may be able to hear and follow the tenor *taleae* of the opening Kyrie without being imbued with medieval theory and sounds. But the isorhythmic technique lends itself to such complications that one may wonder to what extent the elaborate rhythmic structures of the composer were immediately audible even to a listener of his own time and understanding.

One complication can be brought about by increasing the length of a *talea*. The short and familiar pattern of the third rhythmic mode could be easily perceived in its seven repetitions in the first Kyrie. But the *talea* of the tenor in the Christe, for instance, lasts seven long measures, which are repeated three times in the course of the movement. In the second Kyrie, eight measures pass before the tenor repeats the same rhythmic unit; and in the climactic closing Kyrie, fourteen. The internal rhythmic structure of the last example is so irregular and yet so full of delicate correspondences that the ear will hear the structural repetition with the difficulty that the eye will encounter in seeing certain sculptural details high up in the vault of a Gothic cathedral.

The mere length of the basic rhythmic unit provides a relatively minor complication to its easy aural recognition. The relationship of rhythmic to melodic repetition in medieval music is so foreign to a twentieth-century ear and mind that a particular explanation becomes necessary. Melodic repetition is a basic element of almost all music. A composer states a theme and then pleases us by repeating it. We can go as far as to say that the listener depends on melodic repetitions to recognize the shape and the intentions of a musical movement. In the Star-spangled Banner, for instance, the melody of the first couplet (up to the words "at the twilight's last gleaming,") is exactly repeated by the immediately following second couplet ("Whose broad stripes and bright stars," until "were so gallantly streaming?"). The melodic notes of these couplets are identical, and so are

follow their own organization. Nor does the length of *talea* or *color* in one voice necessarily coincide with that of any other voice. An ear trained in the middle of the twentieth century listens for rhythmic and melodic correspondences between the various voices of a composition. But in a fourteenth-century composition one encounters in the place of these correspondences a maximum independence of the participating elements. In the opening Kyrie of Machaut's Mass, for instance, the *talea* of the tenor is four measures long; that of the contratenor, twelve. The internal rhythms are different, and there is no trace of melodic imitation or transfer from one voice to the other. Nor do the upper two voices appear in the least influenced by the rhythmic and melodic material of the tenor and contratenor.

If the patient reader of these lines will experience difficulties in imagining clearly Machaut's complex isorhythmic technique, he may be assured that the most attentive audience of the score will experience similar difficulties in hearing in detail the resulting structure. Machaut's compositions have been praised as ingenious by some and condemned as "paper music" by others. The controversy has evoked many divergent opinions. One of the most recent critics of Machaut, Sarah Jane Williams, insists that isorhythm in most Machaut works, whatever its intellectual distinction, is directly perceptible to the ear. She enumerates various reasons for the tendency to interpret isorhythm as "purely abstract." It is a technique that disappeared with the Middle Ages and that is almost completely unfamiliar today. Many people today are conditioned to listen to the melodic rather than to the rhythmic cohesion of a composition. There are also semantic difficulties; for attempts to describe the technique in words (as we have done) can at best remain suggestive. Williams believes that careful study and repeated performances will overcome the difficulty of following the unfamiliar style. "What at first may be perceived only by an abstract analysis, is soon felt and heard by the listener who becomes at all familiar with the work. The musician who takes the trouble to familiarize himself with Machaut . . . will . . . begin to hear repeated rhythmic patterns which he had hitherto only seen."[45] Nor is Williams alone in her conviction. Richard Hoppin, delivering a paper at a meeting of the American Musicological Society in Austin in 1949 on "Rhythm as a Structural Device in the Motet Around 1400," stated emphatically that, particularly in the generation after Machaut, the *taleae* were so carefully built and clearly defined that the structural "repetitions can scarcely have been missed by even the dullest listener."[28]

The truth of these assertions each listener must find out for himself. There are scholars who judge isorhythm as a purely abstract, intellectual principle which cannot be perceived by the ear. Most of them belong to the generation that rediscovered the music of the Middle Ages in the period following the first World War. Rudolf Ficker, writing for the *Musical Quarterly* in October 1929, finds in the entire history of music hardly an example in which the constructive energy of tectonics attained to such a degree of rigidity as in the isorhythmic compositions of Machaut and his contemporaries. "Of their technical refinements, however, the hearer perceives nothing," he concludes after studying and performing many of them.[15] Heinrich Besseler, in his standard volume on the music of the Middle Ages and the Renaissance, doubts the immediate dynamism of an isorhythmic work. He hears neither the swell of an inner development, nor the drive of thematic progressions, nor the tension of contrasting degrees of loudness and tempo. He considers isorhythm an apotheosis of the ancient faith in the mystery of number, which holds together all things beneath their sensual appearances. The isorhythmic periods, in their strict uniformity, symbolize to him the eternal recurrence of similar and static forces.[3] There is a tradition of relating isorhythm to Neo-Pythagorean and oriental number speculation.[14]

In a similar spirit, Manfred Bukofzer expresses his thoughts: "To retain a certain rhythmic scheme in the various parts of a composition actually meant to keep the same numerical proportion. The musical composition was outlined according to the same rules as was mediaeval architecture. The ground plan of a cathedral obeyed certain laws of proportion, the secrets of which were anxiously guarded by the craftschools . . . Numerical proportion supplied, as it were, the formula of the universe, comprehensible to the intellect alone. The human senses such as the eye and the ear perceive things as unrelated to each other, but the intellect provides the unifying reduction to numerical proportions. The isorhythmic motet, thus, corresponds to human experience in life: the single isorhythmic periods seem different for the ear though they are based on an identical numerical scheme. Thus, the motet represented another device allegorizing the universe."[5]

Gombosi pleads for both sides of the question by distinguishing two principal factors in Machaut's planning. "One appeals to the senses. It manifests itself in the angular and nervous rhythmic motifs rubbing against each other and following each other in regular alternation of uneven metric units from accent to accent. There is no continuum of a 'natural,' physical, bodily movement upon the pattern of which it could be fashioned. Rather it has a capricious, effeminate, and fantastic quality that reflects, with a high degree of stylization, the wonders of the perceptible world. It is worldly.

"The other factor is entirely outside of the sensuous. It concerns itself with the higher order of metric units and lines by bringing them into a complex system of symmetries. It transgresses the proper limits and limitations of music as a perceptible order of tones, and acquires an abstract spatial quality. It mirrors a world outlook that is idealistic and transcendental, mystic and hieratic, Gothic and scholastic. It is other-worldly."[19]

The two apparently opposite interpretations can be reconciled. Isorhythmic patterns will come to life in the hands of a creative composer and will remain on paper in the hands of an unimaginative one. One may remember a similar dispute concerning the writing of fugues; but Bach's *Art of Fugue* and Beethoven's Opus 133 are not mathematical exercises.

We may conclude this controversy by suggesting that a

musician does not hear physically but spiritually. What is meant is not so much a cryptic speculation as a statement of fact. If we hit two notes on a piano—let us say, *c* and *g*, the beginning of "Twinkle, twinkle, little star"—we call the resulting interval a fifth. Actually, what we hear on the piano is hardly ever a fifth. Physically, the two notes will be either too far apart or too close together because a piano is seldom exactly in tune; and even a freshly tuned instrument will produce a flat fifth because of the so-called "temperament" of a keyboard. Spiritually, however, we recognize the fifth immediately because the phenomenon, out of tune as it is, corresponds to the *a priori* norm which we carry in us. It is precisely the pre-existence of this norm in us that helps us select and organize among the infinite possibilities of physical sound combinations those that are aesthetically meaningful. The argument about the physical audibility of a complex isorhythmic structure may resolve itself by the recognition that Machaut's Gothic devices, whether they are directly perceived by the listener or only slowly isolated by the scholar, would not have effected persuasion and pleasure in the fourteenth century as well as six hundred years later if they did not meet an inner demand, and did not correspond to a psychic form, of man.

At the beginning of this chapter we have stated that Machaut holds together certain movements of the Mass by utilizing not only isorhythmic structure but also a *cantus firmus*. Like many technical and scholarly terms, this one is Latin. The principle is simple enough. The composer begins his work with a fixed melody, *cantus firmus*, which is held in very long, drawn-out notes by one of the lower voices. From the act of "holding" the fixed melody, that voice has been named "tenor" (Latin *tenere*, to hold). The notes of the tenor are prolonged to such an extent that the melodic cohesion is felt rather than heard by the listener. The structural unity of the *cantus firmus* provides the steady framework upon which the upper voices may be set in quicker and freer motion. Johannes de Grocheo, a music theorist writing at the beginning of the century in which Machaut lived, calls the tenor "that part over which all others are constructed." He compares it to the foundation of a building; it regulates the other voices and determines their extent, "as a bone structure does."[46] The long duration of each *cantus firmus* tone invites instrumental participation or execution.

The mere description of a musical fact will arouse little sympathy; but sympathy may be increased by an understanding of the historical and psychological forces behind the fact. Music for the first thousand years after Christ, one remembers, was primarily vocal and fundamentally monodic. The idea of hearing two or more different melodies at the same time was foreign to the needs and the imagination of man, although the possibility of simultaneously plucking two strings on an instrument certainly lay within reach and doubtless must have been occasionally realized. Gregorian chant formed the written-down musical treasure of the early Middle Ages. It supplied the material for the initial experiments of polyphony, i.e., of writing for two and more voices. When men and women, or adult men and boys, sing the same melody, they are apt to do so at the octave: all sing the same tones but in a different range. Occasionally, a participant may trace the original melody at a slightly less consonant interval. The fifth has been favored by natural reasons. One can hear a melody in parallel fifth today in situations that approximate the "primitiveness" of earlier centuries. There are always some members of a Sunday morning congregation that audibly sing the hymn tune a fifth away from the main line; and children often follow the same practice in common vocal enterprises. Intervals other than the fifth may be used to the same purpose by more sophisticated groups. The fourth seems to have prevailed in Italy and southern France, while the fifth along with the more dissonant intervals of third and sixth regulated the early polyphonic efforts of northern France, England, and Scandinavia. The choice of interval—fifth, fourth, third, or sixth—has given rise to a speculation on a basic difference between various spheres of civilization.[41] Common to all incipient polyphony is the simultaneous projection of the same given melody by two parallel voices. This kind of singing was called *organum*.

Slow tempo was characteristic of *organum*. The practical consideration for the difficulty of executing the new technique would make us believe so even without the testimony of a ninth-century handbook, the *Musica Enchiriadis*. We may now easily assume that the two voices did not always stay exactly together. The lighter of the two singers, or the more courageous, or the more imaginative, or the more soloistically inclined would embellish his long notes by

quick turns, fast passages, and vocal ornaments until it
gained a pseudo-independence from the steady melody, the
cantus firmus, of the original. The cohesion between the
two voices was preserved by special attention to certain
points of the line where none other than the secure intervals of octave or fifth was tolerated. But the freedom
and, with it, the distance between these points increased.
In a French manuscript of the early twelfth century we find,
among other similar examples, an *organum* for two voices
on the Gregorian melody "Benedicamus Domino."[40] Each of
the eight melody notes for the first word is held and drawn
out in the tenor to such an extent that, before it moves to
the next, the elaborate upper voice has time to sing about
twenty notes against it. The elaboration sounds free; the
old *organum* principle is preserved by adherence to the perfect consonances of octave and fifth whenever the *cantus
firmus* progresses to its next melody tone.

At the end of the century, the technique had become refined and more complex without denying its origin. France
was the center of Western civilization, and Paris was the
center of France. The cornerstone of the Gothic cathedral
dedicated to Notre Dame of Paris was laid in 1163 by Pope
Alexander III. The composition written for the New Year's
Day service thirty-five years later by Perotin, the musical
director of the cathedral, remained famous for centuries and
confirmed the musical leadership of the school of Notre
Dame. The composition in question may serve as an illustration of *cantus firmus* technique before Machaut. It is
built on the Gregorian melody "Sederunt principes," which

unifies and names the whole work. It is written for four voices, of which the lowest holds the *cantus firmus*. The upper three voices are set in contrast against the *cantus firmus*. They move mostly as a unit in the same rhythm and frequently in parallel lines. They sound as if the upper voice of an old *organum* had tripled. Whatever their gain of number and of freedom, the entire composition is held together by the fantastically blown-up notes of the Gregorian tenor. The first two notes of the chant are a minor third apart (as in the opening of Brahms's *Lullaby,* for instance). But before the *cantus firmus* takes the step, each of the upper voices has sung approximately one hundred and fifty notes, and almost two minutes have passed. The whole composition, which lasts about twenty minutes, progresses in this way. A Chicago audience of a few years ago may not have been aware of the melodic unity of the underlying *cantus firmus* but it knew from the impact that the composition somehow hung together (as the writer, then the conductor, can testify).

The thirteenth century, to which Machaut fell heir, seemed less concerned with developing the magnificent fullness of four voices than with establishing the independence of the participating melodies. For this purpose, three voices provided adequate labor. The thirteenth-century motet still needs the foundation of a *cantus firmus*, which is usually Gregorian. But the upper two voices gain an ever increasing freedom, against the tenor and each other; and the *cantus firmus*, though the slowest of the three, projects its tones without exaggerated dilatation in a melodically cohesive manner.

In the fourteenth century, the voices above the tenor were called *motetus* and *triplum*. *Motetus* (French *mot*, word) denotes the presence of a text and hence the performance by a human voice. *Triplum* (Latin, the third) enumerates the addition of a third, highest voice. When the standard setting for three voices is expanded to a setting for four (as is the case in Machaut's Mass), the new voice is heard at the bottom. It is *contra tenorem bassus*, deep compared to the tenor; the medieval term contratenor has now been replaced by bass.

These are some historical facts leading up to Machaut's *cantus firmus* technique. Lest one minimize the technical accomplishments of a long-gone era, the psychological value of a *cantus firmus* must be appraised.

In a period when composers began exploring the realm of polyphony, they might easily have lost themselves in the new wilderness without some firm guidance by a traditional melody. The concept of several simultaneous melodies is one of the most extraordinary accomplishments of man, comparable to little else. One must bear in mind that for thousands of years people in all countries, on all continents, had contentedly listened to the natural flow of a single line. We take the four-part setting of a church hymn or the piano arrangement of a popular song for granted without always remembering the relative recency of the phenomenon, the ingenuity of the idea, and the toil of generations of composers toward its technical perfection. In the freshly gained freedom, a firm limitation was necessary. The need of limitation in any artistic endeavor has been amply discussed in the course of this book. The value of the specific limitation set by a *cantus firmus* to a medieval composition can be measured by the realization that the first polyphonic composers had nothing to hold on to, not even a tradition.

The presence of a *cantus firmus* immediately solved the problem of unity and, if desired, that of structure. However the experimental second and third voices struggled, the composition cohered by force of the continuous flow of the known and standardized tenor. Beginning and end were given by the sanctified scope of the Gregorian melody. So were the points of consonance and the stretches of dissonance, the qualities of rest and tension. And even particles of the melodic substance, perhaps motifs but certainly crests and troughs, helped determine the contours of the upper voices.

In his concern for unity, beginning and end, and tension and relaxation, the medieval composer might pay his respects to Aristotle. By deriving these gains from the firm basis of a given Gregorian chant, he paid his respects to the Holy Roman Church. He depended on the Church, which, at the time Notre Dame was built, supported and cultivated polyphonic writing decisively more than did the contemporary secular aristocracy. Troubadours and trouvères continued to sing and play their monodic lines long after cathedrals resounded with the polyphonic masterpieces of Perotin. The political advantage of a Gregorian *cantus firmus* does not belittle the artistic one. The repeated edicts and bulls of the Church testify to the tenuous state of the new art. A traditionally sanctified tenor melody provided a secure religious as well as musical foundation. The particular loan from the Gregorian treasure could even serve to convey a hidden meaning, so welcome to the symbolic attitude of the Gothic age. In Machaut's Motet No. 23, for instance, the *cantus firmus* on the words "Ad te suspiramus" ("We sigh toward thee") stems from the antiphon *Salve regina*, thus confirming the prayer to the Virgin in the upper voices. In another Motet (No. 4), the hopeful lyrics of a lover ("De Bon Espoir") find support by a *cantus firmus* borrowed from the Introit "Domine, in tua misericordia speravi"—a transfer of the same basic emotion, hope, into a different sphere.

The circumstantial description of some properties of isorhythm and of a *cantus firmus* is inevitable in an argument devoted to Machaut. He did not write many compositions that are devoid of either; and his Mass, the center of our attention, is hardly comprehensible without reference to these particular technical devices.

In the course of our description, the isorhythmic structure of the first portion of the Mass (Kyrie—Christe—Kyrie) has served as an illustration. The cohesion of that portion is reinforced by the presence of a Gregorian *cantus firmus* in the tenor, the Kyrie melody *Cunctipotens genitor deus (in festis duplicibus)*. "This principal part," in the words of Johannes de Grocheo, "must be formed first of all because with its help all others can then be formed, just as nature in the creation of living beings first forms the principal parts,

namely, heart, liver, brains, and with their help then forms
the others."[46] We may assume that Machaut composed the
opening movement by first borrowing and setting down the
liturgical melody of a Kyrie that had been standardized by
Pope Gregory I three quarters of a millennium earlier and
that was consequently familiar to most churchgoers. It can
be found today in Mass IV in the Vatican Edition. Machaut
used the Gregorian melody in its entirety, outlining, as it
were, the ground plan. Then the Gregorian melody with
slight modifications at two cadences was methodically and
artfully cut up into shorter and precisely defined rhythmical
units, the *taleae.* The groundwork of the tenor was cemented
by the co-ordinated structure of the contratenor. Above this
doubly solid foundation, the two upper voices, motetus and
triplum, could now swing out in freer and quicker curves.

We have dealt at great length with the Kyrie without in-
tending to allot comparable space and time to the subsequent portions of the Mass. There is a double advantage to
this method. Thorough concentration on a limited area
often yields the deepest insights, which soon and easily become applicable to other situations. Melville's intense focus
on a white whale opens the whole world. The other advantage lies in sparing the reader a tedious translation of note
after note into word after word. The description of one
musical movement may acquaint one with certain unfamiliar
devices and may whet one's taste for a complete musical experience. Exposure to both a technical analysis and an acous-
tical realization of the score is available to the reader outside
the circumscribed intentions and covers of this book.

The Gloria and the Credo have much in common. There seems to be a tradition linking these two movements into a musical pair, paralleled by a similar unification of the Sanctus and Agnus Dei.[6] Some reasons for the pairing of the Gloria and Credo portions doubtless lie in certain inherent qualities of the liturgical texts. These portions, built in the manner of a psalmody, are the longest of the *ordinarium missae* and therefore resist a leisurely melismatic treatment. Nor are certain devout enumerations in either movement conducive to a free musical outpour ("Laudamus te. Benedicimus te. Adoramus te. Glorificamus te." And the long list of articles of the creed). The music for both movements, incidentally, begins with an intonation by the celebrating priest; and the composition proper continues with the second half of the respective sentences. (In performances, the intonation must be supplied from the *Liber Usualis*.) In any case, the Gloria and Credo of Machaut's Mass are the only portions that are neither isorhythmic nor based on a *cantus firmus*. The four voices move mostly in uniform rhythm. The effect is that one hears not so much independently organized lines but rather a succinct recitation of syllable after syllable in blocklike chords. This kind of writing is reminiscent of a style that was familiar to the old Notre Dame school, a century and more before Machaut, under the technical name of *conductus*. This external reminiscence has been responsible for branding the two movements, and indirectly the entire Mass, as archaic. While the observation may be correct, one may just as easily speculate about the modernism as about the archaism of the Gloria and Credo.

Attesting to the latter is the atmosphere in which the strong words of John XXII against the "new school" mingled with an awareness that there was really no coherent tradition to polyphonic religious music. Machaut, a professional servant of the Church himself, might have attempted to make at least one bow in the direction of Avignon. Like other composers of his century who wrote polyphonic religious movements, he could have chosen a secular type of musical structure for the Gloria and Credo, the fashionable ballade, for instance. But he preferred, in fact, a type in which the liturgical texts could be clearly recited without becoming obscured by polyphony and melismas. The payment of a debt to the purely religious sphere is here not so obvious as in the movements erected on a Gregorian tenor; but the *conductus* had once been devoted primarily to religious expression in music, whatever Machaut's knowledge of this historical fact might have been.

The characterization of a work as "modern" contains the hazard of ambivalence. What sounds startling at the first moment might quickly turn dated. Looking at the Mass with a historical eye at the distance of six hundred years, we sense a connection with the *conductus* style of still two hundred years earlier and are tempted to call the Gloria and Credo archaic. Trying to hear the Mass with the sensitivity and conditioning of a musical ear of the fourteenth century, we wonder at the modernity of precisely these two portions. The absence of both isorhythm and of a *cantus*

firmus creates a freedom that transcends the Gothic structures of the other portions of the Mass. Machaut rises above
the limitations set by the circumscribed style of his period
and finds himself bound by nothing short of his original
imagination. Had anyone before him dared interrupt the
insistent flow of the Credo by amazing slow sounds at the
one spot when the Virgin Mary is mentioned? The phrase
"ex Maria virgine" is thereby thrown into high relief, in
appropriate correspondence to Machaut's naming the work
(in the excellent manuscript formerly owned by the Marquis
Melchior de Vogüé) "La Messe de Nostre Dame." The ex-
pressiveness of the device made it sound modern to the congregation that first heard it in Paris. The same congregation
in the middle of the miseries of the Hundred Years' War,
also understood the rare emphasis, by an identical device, on
the exclamation "Et in terra pax"—"Peace on earth." The
sudden long holds on each syllable are reserved for these two
places and the two direct invocations of "Jesu Christe" in
the Gloria.

There are other "modern" features of a purely technical
kind in these two movements. Repeatedly, sentences are
separated from one another by a flurry of the two lower
voices, which assumes the role of a short instrumental inter-
lude. In both the Gloria and Credo of the Mass by Machaut,
these instrumental interludes become sharply discernible
factors in the over-all organization, which, it has been as-
serted, proceeds on the plan of very free strophic variations.[19]
This concept is anything but archaic. An isolated setting of
the Credo by Bartholino of Padua in the late fourteenth

century takes up the idea.[43] In the Credo of a Mass (K.192) composed four hundred years after Machaut, Mozart employs a recurrent two-measure phrase at similar structural points, and the intermediate sections can just as rightly be called free strophes. We are not attempting to establish a connection between Machaut and Mozart but rather to give a taste of the modernism of Machaut's mind. He was a mature man and composer at the time he wrote the Mass. Whatever the exact date of the composition, it lies doubtless around the center of the century, when Machaut had produced almost all of his motets and had entered upon his maturest experiments. Toward the end of the century, the freedom found by Machaut in the movements under discussion became the up-to-date manner of many French and Italian composers. Ludwig describes a Gloria recorded in a manuscript in Modena [lat. 568] as following the "modern" technique of the "fuga," closely associated with Italian hunting songs and containing, below a canon between two singers, a free instrumental voice.[27]

The pairing of the Gloria and Credo portions finds its analogy in the pairing of the Sanctus and Agnus' Dei portions.[6] This pair, like the preceding one, hangs together not so much by the specific execution of detail but rather by the general spiritual attitude. Composers two generations after Machaut sensed this cohesion when, neglecting to profit from Machaut's idea of a cyclic Mass, they contributed to the liturgy by musically unified Gloria-Credo or Sanctus-Agnus Dei pairs. Machaut's Mass, from the "Amen" phrase of the Credo to the end, is again built on isorhythm and a *cantus firmus.* The origin of the latter in the Sanctus and Agnus Dei confirms the connection of the pair: both *cantus firmi* are derived from the same Gregorian Mass (XVII in the Vatican Edition), for the Sundays of Advent and Lent. In each movement the isorhythmic flow, moreover, commences only after passing through the portal, as it were, of the majestically free opening invocation.

Machaut's treatment of the Agnus Dei as compared to that of the closing Kyrie affords a good example of his ingenious fantasy. In each case the problem is similar but Machaut's solutions differ. A sentence is repeated three times. Here it is an invocation to the Lamb of God; there, to the Lord. Here the double prayer, "Have mercy on us," is widened the third time to "Give us peace." There the supplication for mercy returns unaltered three times. Yet we remember that Machaut intensified the third and last "Kyrie" exclamation by expanding it beyond the scope of the preceding two. The resulting form can be symbolized by the letters *a a b*. This organization would fit even more naturally the text of the Agnus Dei, which introduces the new idea of peace in the third repetition. But Machaut, while intent on avoiding the mechanical triplication of the identical musical setting, is apparently also eager to break away from the pattern set by the Kyrie. He expands one of the Agnus Dei supplications, but it is the second rather than the expected third. The straying from the text nets him a fresh musical structure. The prayer for peace is repeated over the music of the first prayer for mercy, and the resulting form, *a b a*, becomes symmetrical around a center rather than open at the end. There is something uniquely touching about this treatment when after the musically intensified reiteration of "miserere nobis," the final outpour of "dona nobis pacem" humbly returns to the initial music.

Technically, the expansion of the second Agnus Dei is gained by a different rhythmic partition of the same Gregorian melody in the tenor. The *talea* of the first Agnus Dei is seven measures long, and two appearances around a conspicuous chord in the exact center fill the entire section. The *talea* of the second Agnus Dei extends over three measures, and six repetitions of the shorter but more emphatically profiled rhythmic group maintain the over-all symmetry around the center column.

All polyphonic Masses composed after Machaut end with the Agnus Dei. The closing phrase of the service, "Ite, missa est. Deo gratias," "Go, the Mass is over. Thanks be to God," is now chanted by the priest and his server at the altar. To later composers primarily concerned with expression, the factual dismissal of the congregation may have sounded like a musical letdown after the intensely personal and meaningful prayer for mercy and peace. Machaut, one realizes, would not recognize this argument. His setting of the Ite Missa Est concludes the Mass cycle with an exquisitely concise movement, in which a quaternary principle of structure, as in the ogive of a Gothic vault, increases the firmness and fancy of his intent on the foundation of a seven-measure *talea*.

The fate and the historical position of Machaut's Mass are commensurate with its musical values. Tradition has elevated the significance of the Mass by asserting that it was written for, and first performed at, the coronation of Charles V in Notre Dame of Paris in 1364. The association of Machaut's Mass with a festive occasion of supreme political significance indicates the respect in which the composition was held by subsequent generations, although the tradition is not based on any particular evidence. The Mass was probably composed one or two decades before the coronation. In any case, it is the earliest complete polyphonic setting of the *ordinarium missae* known to be written by one man. Masses before Machaut were either purely Gregorian, i.e., for one voice only; or, occasionally, they were put together from individual polyphonic movements written at different periods by different hands. The conception of the Mass as a homogeneous work of art must be credited to Machaut. The idea is original and daring, for it is not necessarily contained in the liturgy. The normal structure of the Mass consists of eighteen separate items, of which some are recited or said (Lesson, Gospel, e.g.) and some sung (Introit, Kyrie, Gradual, etc.). But the latter are scattered throughout the service, separated by nonmusical stretches, and only about one half of them, the *ordinarium missae*, remain constant in the revolution of the Church year. The composition of these constant portions, as carried out by Machaut before anyone else, is the result of conceiving across all nonmusical barriers the possibility of unification. In this sense, the accomplishment is both imaginative and heroic.

On its relation to the history of the period, Gustave Reese, of New York University, sheds a clear light: "Outstanding as this Mass is, sacred music obviously constitutes a com-

paratively small part of Machaut's output. In this respect,
he seems to be a true child of his century. In both French
and Italian 14th-century manuscripts, secular music occupies
the chief attention of composers. This is perhaps the result
of the famous bull of Pope John, issued in the year 1324/5
at Avignon, banning from the church service not only the
addition of motetus and triplum parts to the plainsong but
practically all kinds of polyphony. It seems quite clear, however, that this bull did not fully achieve its ends over any
wide area . . . Composers continued to write polyphonic
music for liturgical use. But the edict may have acted as a
partial check, if not as a complete one, thus diverting the
main flow of musical creation into secular channels. In the
vicinity of Avignon itself, the effect evidently did not last
very long."[40] Nor did the bull stop Machaut from adding
motetus and triplum parts to the plainsong. The canon of
Rheims, the lover of Toute-Belle, had received absolution
for greater sins. But the fact remains that the Mass is the
only significant religious composition in Machaut's output.

We know today of six medieval manuscripts that contain
the music. The work was still performed in the sixteenth
century,[40] when Josquin des Prez could have heard it, trans-
mitting its spirit to the modern age. After a few centuries
of oblivion, a complete performance took place in Paris
at the church of St. Anthony of Padua in 1936; another
one, shortly thereafter at the more fashionable church of
the Madeleine. America first heard the score in 1951, when
choirs in New York in March (under Paul Boepple) and
Chicago in April (under Siegmund Levarie) experienced and

proved the vitality of the music; the New York performance has since become available on records. The score could not have been transformed into actual sound without the ready availability of several printed editions. For six hundred years after Machaut wrote the Mass, it was never printed. Since the war, three modern editions have appeared on the market. The long delay of the publication is tinged with dramatic irony. In 1927, the brilliant German musicologist Friedrich Ludwig began issuing in print the complete musical works of Machaut. The complete poetic works had been published at the beginning of the century in Paris by Ernest Hoepffner after isolated reprints had begun to appear as early as 1849; but literary criticism had not paid much attention to Machaut's musical facets. Ludwig published three volumes, containing most of Machaut's secular works. The Mass was intended for the fourth volume. Ludwig died in 1930, his prepared copy of the Mass at a point from which Breitkopf and Härtel, who had for decades distinguished themselves as publishers of standard editions of old masters, could proceed without his help. Before leaving the publisher's rooms, the whole printing—copy, plates, and all—was destroyed by an Allied bombardment of Leipzig. When three scholars in Europe exerted their best efforts immediately after the war to fill the painful gap by publications of their own, the most reliable of the original sources, the so-called Vogüé manuscript, had mysteriously disappeared. The confusion of the postwar years in Europe may have accounted for the sudden unavailability of a manuscript that, after waiting securely for six hundred years,

vanished precisely at the moment when it was to be returned
to life. The three scholars had to base their editions of
Machaut's Mass on less trustworthy and often conflicting
sources. Then in January 1953, the Vogüé manuscript sud-
denly appeared at an exhibition of medieval and Renaissance music manuscripts at the Toledo Museum of Art in
Ohio. Mr. Beverly Barksdale, who arranged the exhibition,
had called on the art dealers Wildenstein and Company, New
York, to see if they might contribute anything of importance.
Wildenstein graciously offered the Machaut volume and had
it flown over from Paris. A photograph of the opening pages
of the Mass (with the incipit line, "Ci commence La Messe
de Nostre Dame") can be seen in the September 1953 issue
of *Notes* (p. 564), accompanying an article by Mr. Barksdale
on music exhibitions. A letter from Mr. Georges Wildenstein contains the information that he bought the manuscript directly from the Vogüé family "about twenty or
twenty-five years ago" and that it has been in his possession
since that time. By the end of 1953, the manuscript was
still in his collection in New York.

Of the three modern editions referred to, the latest is also
the best. The American Institute of Musicology in Rome en-
trusted Guillaume de Van, formerly of the Bibliothèque
Nationale of Paris and originally a native of Memphis,
Tennessee, with the edition. When he died in 1949, he had
the satisfaction of knowing that his name was appended to
a most handsome, legible, and conscientious volume. Critical
comments and an exhaustive bibliography guide the reader
along the way. So does the adherence to a typographical de-

vice first used by Ludwig, namely, to profile the isorhythmic periods by corresponding arrangements on the printed page.

One year before de Van's edition, there appeared two others—one in France and one in Belgium. Jacques Chailley, choirmaster of the Psallette de Notre-Dame in Paris, prepared a score intended for the performer who is innocent of fourteenth-century problems. Chailley's personal advice often overshadows Machaut's original score. The edition by Armand Machabey, who is one of the world's leading experts on Machaut's music, takes a middle position between the other two, and for this reason might be most satisfactory to the interested but not overly critical layman. The old clefs have been exchanged for the modern G and F clefs. A reduction for keyboard of the score facilitates the reading, although not necessarily the hearing, of the music and may be used to prop a faltering chorus perplexed by the strange style.

What does Machaut mean to us in the twentieth century? Some observed reactions are worth recording. The members of the Collegium Musicum at the University of Chicago were well versed in old music when they began working on the Mass. They had performed Perotin and Dufay, and they could sing Josquin des Prez by sight. The initial difficulty of becoming acquainted with Machaut's idiom was supreme and without parallel. For about two full rehearsals, nobody really heard what was happening and nobody was free of bewilderment—although the separate intervals and lines are not particularly difficult to sing. But then came the moment when everything seemed to clear up and fall into place. After a few months, students walking across the campus were caught whistling some of the phrases.

This experience was duplicated by a well-known concert artist who happened to hear the final rehearsal and the performance. He was first shocked to the point of remaining disturbed in his own activities. The second hearing gave him satisfaction. He later contemplated the possibilities (and obvious difficulties) of incorporating some Machaut compositions in his own concert repertoire.

In general, two reactions will be found among modern listeners. It is possible to gain pleasure and instruction from the mere archaic flavor of old music. The perspective of history lends piquancy to the experience. The limitation of this approach was felt by a performer (who had sung many Machaut works) when he decided to substitute modern instruments for the quaint viols, lutes, and recorders that would provide a more authentic accompaniment. He sensed that the apparent eccentricity might tend to distract the listeners from the essential qualities of the music.

The other possible approach to Machaut is to listen for the direct appeal of his music. Written for human ears, the Mass contains powerful melodic phrases and singular rhythms that can arouse our emotions. The original force of Machaut's spirit can reach us, projecting the artistic accomplishment without depending on elements of quaintness. There lies great satisfaction in one's direct response to another human spirit. We gain strength from the recognition that such response can stay alive across six hundred years and more.

Bibliography

ONLY WORKS used in this book are listed. The interested reader will easily find additional information in the editions of Machaut's poetic works by Hoepffner (No. 32, below) and musical works by Ludwig (No. 28). Three more recent publications (all easily available) contain a wealth of material: Huizinga (No. 24) has given us new insights into the life and spirit of the Middle Ages; Reese (No. 40) covers the music of the same period; and Williams (No. 45) concentrates on Machaut himself. Her dissertation represents the most extensive study of Machaut's music yet written in English, and to her spade work we are greatly indebted.

The controversy about the historical background of the Mass does not lie within the scope of this book. The discussion at the beginning of the third chapter follows in general the authority of Peter Wagner (No. 44).

Most translations (and occasional condensations) in the text are by the author, who would have gladly used the English version of Huizinga, *Waning of the Middle Ages* (London, 1924), if it were not unfortunately incomplete.

Of the bracketed numbers after a title, the one before the colon refers to the page of this book where the reference occurs; the one after the colon, to the page of the source. Several references on the same page are listed in the order in which they occur.

1. ADORNO, T. W. "On Popular Music," *Studies in Philosophy and Social Science*, IX/1 (1941), 17-48. [46:17 f.]
2. AQUINAS, THOMAS. *Summa theologica*. [22:I,q.xxxix,art.8.31, 54:II/2, q.xci,art.2]
3. BESSELER, HEINRICH. *Die Musik des Mittelalters und der Renaissance*. Wildpark-Potsdam, 1931. [88:133]
4. BUEIL, JEAN DE. *Le Jouvencel*. Ed. Camille Favre & Léon Lecestre. 2 vols. Paris, 1887-89. [5:I,19]
5. BUKOFZER, MANFRED. "Speculative Thinking in Mediaeval Music," *Speculum*, XVII (1942), 165-80. [25:168. 89:180]

6. ———. *Studies in Mediaeval and Renaissance Music.* New York, 1950. [79:218. 99:219 ff. 102:219]

7. CARLYLE, THOMAS. *Collected Works.* London: Chapman and Hall, 1870. [15:XXI,172]

8. *Chronique des Quatre Premiers Valois (1327-1393).* Ed. Siméon Luce. Paris, 1862. [6:16;54 ff.]

9. COUSSEMAKER, EDMUND DE (ed.). *Scriptorum de musica medii aevi nova series.* 4 vols. Paris 1864-76. [84:III,225]

10. DELACHENAL, R. *Histoire de Charles V.* 5 vols. Paris, 1909-31. [15:I,23]

11. DENT, EDWARD J. "Social Aspects of Music in the Middle Ages," *Oxford History of Music,* Intr. vol. (London, 1929), 184-221. [25:188. 33:192 f.]

12. DESCHAMPS, EUSTACHE. *Œuvres Complètes.* Ed. Le Marquis de Queux de Saint-Hilaire and Gaston Raynaud. 11 vols. Paris, 1878-1903. [24:VII, 287]

13. FÉTIS, F.-J. *Biographie Universelle des Musiciens.* 2d Ed. 4 vols. Paris 1878-84 [71:I]

14. FICKER, RUDOLF. "Formprobleme der mittelalterlichen Musik," *Zeitschrift für Musikwissenschaft,* VII (1925), 195-213. [88:212]

15. ———. "Polyphonic Music of the Gothic Period," *Musical Quarterly,* XV (1929), 483-505. [88:504]

16. FROISSART, JEAN. *Chroniques.* Ed. Siméon Luce. 12 vols. Paris, 1869-1931. [8:IV,100]

17. FUNCK-BRENTANO, FRANTZ. *The Middle Ages.* Translated from the French by Elizabeth O'Neill. London, 1922. [5:438. 6:473. 7:451;474. 9:482. 10:353]

18. GIBBON, EDWARD. *The History of the Decline and Fall of the Roman Empire.* 3 vols. New York: Random House. [56:I, 715. 78:II, 813, 818]

19. GOMBOSI, OTTO. "Machaut's Messe Notre-Dame," *Musical Quarterly,* XXXVI (1950), 204-24. [89:223 f.]

20. GROSSMANN, WALTER. *Die einleitenden Kapitel des Speculum Musicae.* Leipzig, 1924. [30:91]

21. GUIFFREY, JULES. *Inventaires de Jean Duc de Barry (1401-1416).* 2 vols. Paris, 1894. [16:I,cxliii ff.]

22. HAAS, ROBERT. *Aufführungspraxis der Musik.* Wildpark-Potsdam, 1930. [54:51]

23. HOPPIN, RICHARD H. "Rhythm as a Structural Device in the Motet around 1400," (Abstract), *Journal of the American Musicological Society,* III (1950), 157-8.

24. HUIZINGA, J. *Herbst des Mittelalters: Studien über Lebens- und*

Geistesformen des 14. und 15. Jahrhunderts in Frankreich und in den Niederlanden. 2d Ed. München, 1928. [11:214. 12:210. 13:284;222;226. 17:229 f. 21:162. 22:400. 23:400. 24:300. 32:401; 215 f. 59:50 ff.]

25. KNIGHTON, HENRY. *Chronicon.* Ed. Joseph R. Lumby. 2 vols. London, 1889-95. [7:II,59]

26. LORD, DANIEL. "Something New in Masses," *The Queen's Work,* XXXVII (October, 1944), 5.

27. LUDWIG, FRIEDRICH. "Die mehrstimmige Messe des 14. Jahrhunderts," *Archiv für Musikwissenschaft,* VII (1925), 417-35. [102:423]

28. MACHAUT, GUILLAUME DE. *Musikalische Werke.* Ed. Friedrich Ludwig. 3 vols. Leipzig, 1926-29. [13:III,37 ff.; 62 ff. 16:II,11*. 19:II,32*]

29. ———. *Messe Notre-Dame . . .* Ed. Jacques Chailley. Paris, 1948.

30. ———. *Messe Notre-Dame . . .* Ed. Armand Machabey. Liége, 1948.

31. ———. *La Messe de Nostre Dame.* Ed. G. de Van. Rome, 1949.

32. ———. *Œuvres.* Ed. Ernest Hoepffner. 3 vols. Paris, 1908-21. [8:I, 137 ff. 9:I, xxv; xxxv ff. 14:I, xii ff. 15:I, xxii. 18 f.:I, iii-viii. 20:I, 1-12. 26:II, 125-47]

33. ———. *Le Livre du Voir-Dit . . .* Ed. Paulin Paris. Paris, 1875. [9:136. 16:203. 17:203;95 f.;110. 18:143 ff. 20:69. 22:258. 23:61. 28:69. 29:28]

34. ———. *La Prise d'Alexandre.* Ed. L. de Mas Latrie. Geneva, [1877. 28:35 f.]

35. MARRIOTT, SIR JOHN ARTHUR RANSOME. *A Short History of France.* New York, 1944. [11:90 f.]

36. *Mediator Dei: Encyclical Letter of Pope Pius XII on the Sacred Liturgy.* Vatican Library Translation. Washington, 1947.

37. *Motu Proprio on Sacred Music of Pius X.* Translated by C. J. McNaspy. Toledo: Gregorian Institute of America, 1950. [48:par. 6. 62:pars. 2;5. 63:par. 11c. 64:par.23. 66:par.3]

38. PISAN, CHRISTINE DE. *Le Livre des Fais et Bonnes Meurs du Sage Roy Charles V.* Ed. S. Solente. 2 vols. Paris, 1936 [9:II, 34]

39. PLAMENAC, DRAGAN. "Keyboard Music of the 14th Century in Codex Faenza 117," *Journal of the American Musicological Society,* IV/3 (1951), 179-201. [29:184]

40. REESE, GUSTAVE. *Music in the Middle Ages.* New York, 1940. [93:226. 106:357]

41. SCHNEIDER, MARIUS. *Geschichte der Mehrstimmigkeit.* 2 vols. Berlin, 1934-35.

42. THOMAS, ANTOINE. "Extraits des archives du Vatican pour servir à l'histoire littéraire," *Romania,* X (1881), 321-33. [15:330 ff.]

43. VAN, GUILLAUME DE (ed.). *Les Monuments de l'Ars Nova.* Paris, 1938. [102:I,5-12]

44. WAGNER, PETER. *Geschichte der Messe. I. Teil: bis 1600.* Leipzig, 1913. [73:14 f. 75:15]

45. WILLIAMS, SARAH JANE. *The Music of Guillaume de Machaut.* Unpublished Ph.D. dissertation, Yale University, 1952. Pp. 392. [19:333 f. 24:291. 87:154 ff.]

46. WOLF, JOHANNES. "Die Musiklehre des Johannes de Grocheo," *Sammelbände der Internationalen Musikgesellschaft,* I (1899), 65-130. [91:108. 98-109]

47. WOOLDRIDGE, H. E. *The Oxford History of Music,* I. 2d Ed. London, 1929. [36:294-96]

Records

CHAILLEY, JACQUES. Kyrie, sect. A; Credo, vss. 7-9. *Gramophone* (*Les Maîtres français du Moyen Âge*), No. DB 5118.

DESSOFF CHOIRS (Paul Boepple) Notre Dame Mass. *Concert Hall,* No. CHS 1107.

VAN, GUILLAUME DE. Credo. *Anthologie sonore,* No. 31. Sanctus, Agnus Dei, et Ite. *Ibid.,* No. 32.